CAMBRIDGE LIBRARY COLLECTION

Books of enduring scholarly value

Spiritualism and Esoteric Knowledge

Magic, superstition, the occult sciences and esoteric knowledge appear regularly in the history of ideas alongside more established academic disciplines such as philosophy, natural history and theology. Particularly fascinating are periods of rapid scientific advances such as the Renaissance or the nineteenth century which also see a burgeoning of interest in the paranormal among the educated elite. This series provides primary texts and secondary sources for social historians and cultural anthropologists working in these areas, and all who wish for a wider understanding of the diverse intellectual and spiritual movements that formed a backdrop to the academic and political achievements of their day. It ranges from works on Babylonian and Jewish magic in the ancient world, through studies of sixteenth-century topics such as Cornelius Agrippa and the rapid spread of Rosicrucianism, to nineteenth-century publications by Sir Walter Scott and Sir Arthur Conan Doyle. Subjects include astrology, mesmerism, spiritualism, theosophy, clairvoyance, and ghost-seeing, as described both by their adherents and by sceptics.

Magic and Fetishism

'A pioneer of modern anthropology', A.C. Haddon (1855–1940) contributed to the fields of embryology and evolutionary science before turning his interests to human civilisation and its history. In this work, first published in 1910, Haddon makes use of his wide-ranging knowledge of folk rituals and religious beliefs to introduce readers to basic principles of sympathetic magic, divination, talismanic powers and fetishism. A strong believer in the importance of preserving local religious practices and beliefs, Haddon uses the work to document customs from Britain to West Africa, America to Australia. Topics include forms of contagious magic, premised on a mutual influence between objects; amulets and talismans; magical names and words; and divination. In the second portion of the book, devoted to fetishism, Haddon offers an authoritative description of the fetish as a 'habitation, temporary or permanent, of a spiritual being', establishing basic definitions for an important field of cultural research.

Cambridge University Press has long been a pioneer in the reissuing of out-of-print titles from its own backlist, producing digital reprints of books that are still sought after by scholars and students but could not be reprinted economically using traditional technology. The Cambridge Library Collection extends this activity to a wider range of books which are still of importance to researchers and professionals, either for the source material they contain, or as landmarks in the history of their academic discipline.

Drawing from the world-renowned collections in the Cambridge University Library and other partner libraries, and guided by the advice of experts in each subject area, Cambridge University Press is using state-of-the-art scanning machines in its own Printing House to capture the content of each book selected for inclusion. The files are processed to give a consistently clear, crisp image, and the books finished to the high quality standard for which the Press is recognised around the world. The latest print-on-demand technology ensures that the books will remain available indefinitely, and that orders for single or multiple copies can quickly be supplied.

The Cambridge Library Collection brings back to life books of enduring scholarly value (including out-of-copyright works originally issued by other publishers) across a wide range of disciplines in the humanities and social sciences and in science and technology.

Magic and Fetishism

ALFRED C. HADDON

CAMBRIDGE
UNIVERSITY PRESS

CAMBRIDGE UNIVERSITY PRESS

Cambridge, New York, Melbourne, Madrid, Cape Town,
Singapore, São Paolo, Delhi, Mexico City

Published in the United States of America by Cambridge University Press, New York

www.cambridge.org
Information on this title: www.cambridge.org/9781108044424

© in this compilation Cambridge University Press 2012

This edition first published 1910
This digitally printed version 2012

ISBN 978-1-108-04442-4 Paperback

RELIGIONS ANCIENT AND MODERN

MAGIC AND FETISHISM

MAGIC
AND FETISHISM

By

ALFRED C. HADDON, Sc.D., F.R.S.

UNIVERSITY LECTURER IN ETHNOLOGY, CAMBRIDGE

LONDON

CONSTABLE & COMPANY LTD

10 ORANGE STREET LEICESTER SQUARE W.C.

1910

PREFATORY NOTE

IT is by no means easy to do justice to such a large, comprehensive, and at the same time vague subject as magic in the small compass of a Primer, and part of even that small space had to be devoted to another subject. For sins of omission I must claim this excuse; for sins of commission I claim the indulgence of the reader.

A. C. H.

CONTENTS

MAGIC

MAGIC

I. SYMPATHETIC MAGIC

As knowledge increases, mankind learns more and more about the world and the processes of nature, but even at the present day the vast majority of white men possess only a rudimentary amount of this knowledge; indeed, most so-called educated people have very vague ideas concerning the physical universe in which they live. Such being the case, it is not surprising that primitive peoples have very confused notions concerning these matters, and, as the result of false inductions concerning the causes of phenomena, they seek to accomplish ends by means that we recognise as inadequate. 'It is plain,' as Dr. Jevons points out (36, 33), 'that as long as man is turned loose as it were amongst these innumerable possible causes with nothing to guide his choice, the chances against his making the right selection are considerable.' Further, 'no progress could be made in science until man had distinguished, at any rate roughly, possible from absolutely impossible effects (or causes), and had learned to dismiss from consideration the impossible. It might be expected that experience would suffice of itself to teach man this essential distinction, but the vast majority of the human race have not yet learned from experience that like does not necessarily produce like: four-fifths of mankind, probably, believe in sympathetic magic.'

The instances of sympathetic magic as Dr. Hirn points out (32, 278) are naturally divided into two main classes which, broadly speaking, correspond to the two types of association, contiguity and similarity, and as in psychology it is often difficult to decide whether a given associative process has its origin in a relation of contiguity or in one of similarity, so it is often an open question to which group a given superstition is to be assigned. We will start from the facts that are simpler and easier to explain.

A. Contagious Magic.

1. Sympathetic Magic based on a material connection between things (32, 279) has been aptly termed by Dr. Frazer (21, 77) **Contagious Magic**. All over the world we meet with examples of the belief that objects which were once related to one another retain their connection though they may

be separated, and whatever may happen to one part or object the other part or object is similarly affected; thus, by acting upon a part of a given whole we may influence the whole as well as all its other parts.

This belief explains why a magician, wishing to influence or act upon some particular individual, desires to obtain some portion of his body or something actually connected with him. A few hairs from the beard, a lock of hair, some nail-parings, a drop of blood from the nose which has fallen to the ground, and which has not been rendered impalpable by effacing it with the foot, are used by Basuto sorcerers (10, 277), and indeed by workers of magic everywhere. A few of the examples collected by Mr. Hartland (30, ii. 66) will suffice to demonstrate the universality of this belief. In some parts of England a girl forsaken by her lover is advised to get a lock of his hair and boil it; whilst it is simmering in the pot he will have no rest. In certain parts of Germany and Transylvania the clippings of the hair or nails, as well as broken pieces of the teeth, are buried beneath the elder tree which grows in the courtyard, or are burnt, or carefully hidden, for fear of witches. Patagonians burn the hairs brushed out from their heads, and all the parings of their nails for they believe that spells may be wrought upon them by any one who can obtain a piece of either.

The potency of the hair is shown in the beliefs about the long narrow beaded band which is used to tie up the hair of a Musquakie woman (56, 96, 7). This, though a talisman when first worn, becomes something infinitely more sacred and precious, being transfused with the essence of her soul; any one gaining possession of it has her for an abject slave if he keeps it, and kills her if he destroys it. A woman will go from a man she loves to a man she hates if he has contrived to possess himself of her hair-string; and a man will forsake wife and children for a witch who has touched his lips with her hair-string. The hair-string is made for a girl by her mother or grandmother and decorated with 'luck' patterns; it is also prayed over by the maker and a shaman. The scalp-lock ornament worn by the Musquakie men is kept with great care as it helps to protect the soul. As the tearing out of the scalp-lock makes the soul at its root the slave of the one obtaining it, so the possession of its ornament and shield, which has absorbed some of its essence, gives the possessor the ability to send the rightful owner brain fever and madness (56, 106).

In the South Sea Islands it was necessary to

4

the success of any sorcery to secure something connected with the body of the victim. Accordingly a spittoon was always carried by the confidential servant of a chief in the Hawaiian Islands to receive his expectorations, which were carefully buried every morning. The Tahitians used to burn or bury the hair they cut off, and every individual among them had his distinct basket for food. As Mr. Hartland points out (30, ii. 76), the custom, everywhere practised, of obliterating all trace of the saliva after spitting, doubtless originated in the desire to prevent the use of it for magical purposes, and the same desire led to the extreme cleanliness in the disposal of fouler excreta which is almost universally a characteristic of savages. Thus this belief has been one of the most beneficial of superstitions.

Luck-bags of red cloth, which contain 'the four things of good fortune,' are made by witches in Italy (43, 287), who while sewing it sing an incantation. American Negroes brought over from West Africa the art of making 'luck-balls' or 'cunjerin' bags,' a practice which is kept up to the present day. They are supposed to bring happiness and success in everything the owner undertakes; one made for Charles G. Leland, at the instigation of Miss Owen (57, 173), contained, in addition to knotted threads, a piece of foil to represent the brightness of the little spirit that was going to be in the ball, a leaf of clover *in the place of the hair of the one that is going to own the ball,* and some dust which was designed to blind the eyes of enemies. Miss Owen got the same man, Alexander, the King of the Voodoos, who made the ball for Mr. Leland, to make one for me, and she informed me that 'it was made just like Mr. Leland's with the same words and with the same materials, excepting the clover. This is not the season for clover, *so a fragment of paper, torn from one of your books, represents you.*'

It is not essential that the object to be operated upon should have formed an actual part of a person, for something associated with that person, such as something habitually worn or used, is sufficient, or as in the case of the luck-ball just cited, the association may be as remote as that between an author and a piece of the paper of a book he has published.

Earth from a man's footprints, on account of its close contact with the person, has acquired the virtues of a portion of his body. Widely spread in Germany is the belief that if a sod whereon a man has trodden—all the better if with the naked foot—be taken up and dried behind the hearth or oven, he will parch up with it and languish, or his foot will be withered. He will be lamed, or even killed, by sticking his footprint with nails—coffin nails are the best—or broken glass (30, ii. 78); but these are also the practices of Australian or other savages. To quote only one example from Australia (34, 26), sharp fragments of quartz, glass, bone, or charcoal are buried in the footprints of the victim or in the mark made in the ground by his reclining body. They are supposed to enter the victim, and rheumatic affections are very frequently attributed to them.

Clothes, from their intimate association with the person, have naturally attained a prominent place among the instruments of witchcraft. In Germany and Denmark no portion of a survivor's clothing must on any account be put upon a corpse, else the owner will languish away as it moulders in the grave. To hang rags from the clothing of a dead man upon a vine is to render it barren. 'Probably,' as Mr. Hartland suggests, 'it is only a different interpretation of the same belief which alike in Christian, in Mohammedan, and in Buddhist lands has led to the ascription of marvellous powers to the clothes and other relics of departed saints. The divine power which was immanent in these personages during life attaches not merely to every portion of their bodies but to every shred of their apparel' (30, ii. 90). An illustrative parallel can be taken from the Pacific. The red feathers which adorned the sacred girdle worn by the Tahitian kings were taken from the images of the gods. The girdle 'thus became sacred, even as the person of the gods, the feathers being supposed to retain all the dreadful attributes of power and vengeance which the idols possessed, and with which it was designed to endow the king.' So potent was it that Mr. Ellis says (17, iii. 108) it 'not only raised him to the highest earthly station, but identified him with their gods.'

It is conceivable, as Mr. Hartland suggests (30, ii. 214), that uneducated folk might argue thus: if an article of my clothing in a witch's hands may cause me to suffer, the same article in contact with a beneficent power may relieve pain, restore me to health, or promote my general prosperity. Hence the practice of throwing pins into wells, of tying rags on bushes and trees, of driving nails into trees and stocks, of throwing stones and sticks on cairns, and the analogous practices throughout the world, suggest that they are to be interpreted as acts of ceremonial union

8

with the spirit identified with well, tree, stock, or cairn (30, ii. 228). In the British Islands the sanctity of the well or bush was subsequently annexed by the missionaries who took up their abode beside them, and thus we find the wells or trees called after certain saints and the healing power attributed to the latter, whereas the holiness and efficacy of the wells were in the vast majority of cases, if not in all, pre-Christian (27, 383).

Objects are worn or eaten so that by induction the individual may acquire their properties. Thus the Red Indian hunter (70, 131) wears ornaments of the claws of the grizzly bear, that he may be endowed with its courage and ferocity, and the Tyrolese hunter still wears tufts of eagle's down in his hat, to gain the eagle's keen sight and courage. 'Look,' writes Casalis (10, 271), 'at those strange objects hanging from the necks of our little black friends. There is a kite's foot in order that the poor child may escape misfortune with the swiftness of the kite in its flight. Another has the claw of a lion in order that his life may be as firmly secured against all danger as that of a lion; a third is adorned with the tarsus bone of a sheep, or an iron ring, that he may oppose to evil a resistance as firm as iron,

or as that little compact bone without marrow
which could not be crushed between two stones
without difficulty.'

The eating of certain kinds of food, more
especially of the flesh of animals, would similarly
have a very potent effect; thus among the Dyaks
(65, i. 176), young men sometimes abstain from
eating the flesh of deer, lest they should become
timid. The Abipones of Paraguay (14, 258) 'de-
test the thought of eating hens, eggs, sheep, fish,
or tortoises, imagining that these tender kinds
of food engender sloth and languor in their
bodies and cowardice in their minds. On the
other hand they eagerly devour the flesh of the
tiger [jaguar], bull, stag, boar, anta and tamandua
[ant-eaters], having an idea that, from continually
feeding on these animals, their strength, bold-
ness, and courage are increased.'

Belief in contagious magic leads quite logically
to various revolting practices. In Torres Straits
the sweat of renowned warriors was drunk by
young men, who also ate mixed with their food
the scrapings from the finger-nails of the warriors
which had become saturated with human blood
in order 'to make strong and like a stone; no
afraid' (29, v. 301). The eyes and tongue of a
freshly killed enemy were frequently torn out

and given to lads to make them brave and fearless. The Australian natives believe that a man's fat and his strength and vitality are connected, therefore the wasting of the body and disease are the result of the absence of fat, perhaps to be followed by death. By eating a man's fat, and thus making it part of himself, the black fellow thinks that he also acquires the strength of the deceased. So also they think that human fat brings success in hunting, causes spears which are anointed with it to fly true, or the club to strike irresistible blows. The possession of human fat is, therefore, much desired by these aborigines, especially those who feel age or disease, or who wish to be successful in the magical arts, for it is believed that the spirit of the dead man whose fat has been used will help the charm to act (35, 411, 361). Cannibalism for magical purposes of this sort has probably been extremely common and is possibly at the base of a good deal of anthropophagy.

Very widely spread is the belief that close relatives or even friends are bound together in a sympathetic relation, which is especially manifest on important occasions or at critical times. When a Land Dyak village has turned out for a wild-pig hunt in the jungle, those who remain at home may not touch water or oil with their hands during the absence of their friends, lest the hunters should all become 'butter-fingered,' and the prey so escape them (60, i. 430). It is also recorded from Borneo that when men are on a war expedition, fires are lighted at home, the mats are spread, and the fires kept up till late in the evening and lighted again before dawn, so that the men may not be cold; the roofing of the house is opened before dawn, so that the men may not lie too long and so fall into the enemies' hands (60, ii. 104). Again when a Dyak is out head-hunting, his wife, or, if he is unmarried, his sister, must wear a sword day and night, in order that he may be always thinking of his weapons; and she may not sleep during the day nor go to bed before two in the morning, lest her husband or brother should thereby be surprised in his sleep by an enemy (20, i. 30). Similar instances could easily be multiplied indefinitely from various savage countries, but even in Europe there are not lacking records of a real sympathy between husband and wife, where the former suffers from certain characteristic ailments of the latter (59, 240). There is a very widely spread series of customs based upon the belief that the father and his unborn or newly born child are in such sympathetic relationship that the former has to take all sorts of precautions lest his offspring should in any way be injured. The extreme form this custom takes is for the newly made father to take to his bed and be specially dieted; this occurs in many places, but notably in the East Indian Archipelago and in South America. The custom, which is known as the *Couvade*, is subject to many modifications, which have been tabulated and discussed by Mr. H. Ling Roth (59, 204). Among the Land Dyaks of Borneo the husband of a pregnant woman, until the time of her delivery, may not do work with any sharp instrument, except what may be absolutely necessary for the cultivation of his farm; he may not tie things together with rattans, or strike animals, or fire guns, or do anything of a violent character for fear of injuring the child. Often the men must abstain from certain food lest it should affect the child; thus in Guiana partaking of the Agouti would make the child meagre, or eating a *labba* would make the infant's mouth protrude like the *labba's*, or make it spotted like the *labba*, which spots would ultimately become ulcers (59, 220). Thus the father is frequently debarred from performing many of the usually

13

unconsidered daily acts, lest they should affect the welfare of a child that is newly born or is about to be born; and there is the curious development of the belief of an occult reaction of the expected child on the father, affecting, to take one example, his success in fishing (59, 234).

B. Homœopathic Magic.

2. When man first began to think about the world around him he must have noted (what he, in common with other animals, had unconsciously acted upon in the past) that day and night and the seasons arrived in regular succession, the same stars rose and set, an animal reproduced its own kind, in fact that there was a uniformity in nature. But side by side with these natural sequences there were irregularities. Some days were shorter than others, some were bright, others cloudy, the length and character of the seasons varied from year to year, some stars had a course in the heavens independent of the majority. Again, he might early have noticed that many of these fluctuations in sunshine and rain, in heat and cold, affected him directly or indirectly by influencing vegetation. We need not be surprised, therefore, if he came to the conclusion that it would be better for him

if he exerted himself to regulate matters somewhat, but then the difficulty would arise, what was he to do?

The unenlightened mind does not discriminate between cause and effect, and imagines that as like produces like, so a result can be attained by imitating it. Hence arose **Mimetic or Symbolic Magic**, which, following Dr. Hirn, is better termed **Homœopathic Magic**, which is occult influence based upon a likeness between things (32, 282). On this was founded the mediæval medical theory known as the Doctrine of Signatures, which supposes that plants and minerals indicate by their external characters the diseases which nature intended them to remedy.

It would be easy to give a large number of examples to illustrate homœopathic magic, but a few will suffice. Thus the Euphrasia, or eyebright, was, and is, supposed to be good for the eyes, on the strength of a black pupil-like spot in its corolla (70, 123). The yellow turmeric, or saffron, cured jaundice. The roots of roses or their slips, with their knots removed and set amongst broom, will bring forth yellow roses (47, x. 70).

The influence of homœopathic magic can be traced in beliefs and practices from the lowest savages to civilised nations. The magician who works by similarities makes representations of things or beings, in order to acquire an influence over them. By dramatic or pictorial imitation heavenly bodies are influenced, rain is made, plants and animals are increased, animals enticed to their destruction, human beings acted upon.

When it was wished to cause rain to fall in Murray Island, Torres Straits, the rain-maker scooped a hole in the ground, and lined it with leaves and placed in it a rude stone image of a man which had previously been anointed with oil and rubbed with scented grass; then he poured the decoction of minced leaves of various plants mixed with water over the image—the image being so laid in the hole as to point to the quarter from which the rain was expected. Earth was heaped over the image and leaves and shells placed on the mound, and all the while the rain-maker muttered an incantation in a low sepulchral tone. Four large screens composed of plaited coco-nut leaves were placed at the head, foot, and sides of the grave to represent clouds; on the upper part of each was fastened a blackened oblong of vegetable cloth to mimic a black thunder-cloud, and coco-nut leaves, with their leaflets pointing downwards, were suspended close by to represent rain. A torch was ignited

and waved lengthwise over the grave; the smoke
represented clouds and the flames mimicked light-
ning, and a bamboo clapper was sounded to
imitate thunder.

The rain was supposed to come when the decoction round the image was rotten. The incantation consisted of enumerating various aspects
of certain forms of clouds. Rain could be made
in this manner only by one section of the community, and amongst these one or two men had a
much greater reputation than the others (29, vi.).

This may be taken as an example of a typical
rain-making ceremony, in which all the phenomena of a thunder shower are imitated.

If a native of Mabuiag, in Torres Straits, required rain he went to the rain-maker and asked
him to make some. The latter might reply,
'You go and put some more thatch on your
house and on mine too'; this was to keep out
the forthcoming rain. The rain-maker painted
the front of his body white, and the back black.
This was explained by my informant thus: 'All
along same as clouds, black behind, white he go
first,' or he painted his body with black spots
to make the clouds come separately; when they
congregated, the rain fell. The rain-maker put
'medicine' in his right hand and waved it to-

wards his body and chanted an incantation. To stop the rain the rain-maker put red paint on the crown of his head, to represent the shining sun, and ruddled his body all over. He then lay doubled up and was closely surrounded with three mats, so that no wind could penetrate to him. Finally he burnt some leaves on the sea-shore close to the water, on a rising tide; the smoke represented the clouds, and as it was dissipated so they disappeared, and as the encroaching sea washed away the ashes, so the clouds were scattered (29, v. 350).

In the island of Muralug certain old men could raise a wind by very rapidly whirling a thin bull-roarer attached to a long string. More wind could be obtained by climbing to the top of a tree and performing there. In this case the noise made by the bull-roarer imitated that produced by a gale of wind (29, v. 352).

Examples of the magical increase of plants are found in the 'yam stones' placed in their gardens by various Papuans, which by their rounded shape suggest the actual tubers (28, 202; 29, vi.).

The following instances are culled from that treasury of folk custom and belief—*The Golden Bough*. In Thüringen the man who sows flax carries the seed in a long bag which reaches from his shoulders to his knees, and he walks with long strides, so that the bag sways to and fro on his back. It is believed that this will cause the flax to wave in the wind. In the interior of Sumatra rice is sown by women who, in sowing, let their hair hang loose down their back, in order that the rice may grow luxuriantly and have long stalks. It is commonly believed in Germany and Austria that leaping high in the fields will make the flax or hemp grow tall. A Bavarian sower, in sowing wheat, will sometimes wear a golden ring, in order that the corn may have a fine yellow colour (20, i. 35, 36).

As references are given on pp. 41-44 to magical practices for the increase of animals, further examples need not be added here, their object being to provide plenty of food for the community. It was for the same reason that images of fish, turtle, and dugong were made by the islanders of Torres Straits and taken with them when they went fishing, with the idea that the image lured the real animal to its destruction; and men of the dugong clan who were symbolically decorated made mimetic movements with a dead dugong to constrain others to come and be caught (29, v. 337, 182, and vi.).

The same people used to carve small human

effigies out of thin slabs of wood and coat them with beeswax, or the images were made entirely of beeswax. These figures were treated in various ways for nefarious magic, but always the first action was to call them by the names of the persons who were to be affected by them. If the magician pulled an arm or a leg off the image, the patient felt sore in the corresponding limb, and became ill, and eventually died in great pain; should the magician restore the dismembered limb, the patient would recover. If a magician pricked with the spine of a sting ray an image that had been named, the person indicated would be stung in the same place by a sting ray when he went fishing on the reef (29 v. 324). Analogous customs are to this day practised in Britain. The first example comes from Ross-shire (48, 373). The *corp creagh* is a body of clay rudely shaped into the image of a person whose hurt is desired. After a tolerably correct representation is obtained, it is stuck all over with pins and thorns and placed in a running stream. As the image is worn away by the action of the water the victim also wastes away with some mortal disease. The more pins that are stuck in from time to time the more excruciating agony the victim suffers. Should, however, any wayfarer discover the *corp* in the stream, the spell is broken and the victim duly recovers. From Argyleshire we learn (49, 144) that a long incantation was used as the pins were being put in the clay image, the beginning of which was something to this effect: 'As you waste away, may —— waste away; as this wounds you, may it wound ——.' When it was desired that the person should die a lingering death, care was taken that the pins should not touch where the heart was supposed to be; but when a speedy death was desired, the pins were stuck over the region of the heart. Actual instances of the employment of the *corp chrè* or *corp chreadh*, clay body or clay corpse (as Dr. Maclagan calls it), are given by the two authors last cited, one of which occurred about the year 1899. This practice is merely the continuance of old customs, for 'King James in his *Dæmonology*, says that "the devil teacheth how to make pictures of wax or clay, that by roasting thereof, the persons that they bear the name of may be continually melted or dried away by continual sickness"; and in the eleventh century certain Jews, it was believed, made a waxen image of Bishop Eberhard, set about with tapers, bribed a clerk to baptize it, and set fire to it on the Sabbath, the which image burning away at the middle, the bishop fell grievously sick and died' (70, 124).

Many magical practices and beliefs are difficult to classify as either contagious or homœopathic magic; they may even be a mixture of both. Such is the belief in the power of names or words, talismans and amulets, divination, and various practices of public and private magic. These will be dealt with under separate headings.

II. MAGICAL POWER OF NAMES AND WORDS

A **Name** is considered by backward folk to be part and parcel of a living being, and as magic can be performed on a person through tangible substances that have come into contact with him, so magic can be performed or influence exerted through the utterance of a person's name. In the west of Ireland and in Torres Straits people have refused to tell me their names, though there was no objection to some one else giving me the information; the idea evidently being that by telling their own name to a stranger they were voluntarily putting themselves into the power of that stranger, who, by the knowledge of their name so imparted, could affect them in some way. Over the greater part of America was spread the belief in a personal soul, which is neither the bodily life nor yet the mental power, but a sort of spiritual body. In many tribes, writes Dr. Brinton (7, 277), this third soul or 'astral body' bore a relation to the private personal name. Among the Mayas and Nahuas, it was conferred or came into existence with the name; and for this reason the personal name was sacred and rarely uttered. The name was thus part of the individuality, and through it the soul could be injured. Professor Rhŷs has shown (58, 566-7) from philological evidence, that Aryan-speaking peoples 'believed at one time not only that the name was a part of the man, but that it was that part of him which is termed the soul, the breath of life.' The dislike of hearing their names mentioned is not confined to human beings, for, as is well known, in the British Islands the Fairies have a very strong repugnance to being so called; hence they should be termed the Wee-folk, the Good People, or by other ambiguous terms. Certain Scottish and English fishermen believe that the salmon and pig have a similar objection to being 'named,' but they do not mind being called respectively the 'red-fish' or the 'queer fellow.'

If power can be exerted over men by the use of their names, it is only reasonable to believe that spirits and deities can be similarly influenced. Torres Straits islanders believe that a local bogey or a spirit-girl can be summoned by being mentioned by name (29, v. 14, 86), as the witch of Endor brought up the spirit of Samuel. Dr. Frazer (20, i. 443-6) gives examples to show that people have believed that gods must keep their true names secret, lest other gods or even men should be able to conjure with them; even Ra, the great Egyptian god of the sun, declared that the name given him by his father and mother 'remained hidden in my body since my birth, that no magician might have magic power over me.' This probably was one reason why the real name of supreme Gods was known but to a chosen few; one instance will suffice. To the Mohammedans, Allah is but an epithet in place of the Most Great Name; for, according to a Moslem belief, the secret of the latter is committed to prophets and apostles alone. Another reason is that the utterance of these secret names gives tremendous power, for (42, 273) those who know the Most Great Name of God can, by pronouncing it, transport themselves from place to place at will, can kill the living, raise the dead to life, and work other miracles.

According to Jewish tradition, when Lilith,

POWER OF NAMES

Adam's first wife, refused to yield obedience to him she uttered the Shem-hamphorash, that is, pronounced the ineffable name of Jehovah and instantly flew away. This utterance evidently gave her such power that even Jehovah could not coerce her, and the three angels, Snoi (Sennoi), Snsnoi (Sansennoi), and Smnglf (Sammangeloph), who were sent after her, were contented with a compromise, and Lilith swore by the name of the Living God that she would refrain from doing any injury to infants wherever and whenever she should find those angels, or their names, or their pictures, on parchment or paper, or on whatever else they might be drawn, 'and for this reason,' says a rabbinical writer, 'we write the names of these angels on slips of paper or parchment, and bind them upon infants, that Lilith seeing them, may remember her oath; and may abstain from doing our infants any injury' (1, 165). The custom is still maintained in the east of London of printing portions of Scripture and these three names on pieces of paper, which are placed on the four walls of a room where a baby is expected, where they remain eight days for a boy and twenty days for a girl.

Apart from the coercive power which is attributed to the pronouncing of names, there is an analogous belief in the utterance of words or phrases. Those **Words of Power** have been classed by Mr. Clodd (11, 194) as: (1) Creative Words; (2) Mantrams and their kin; (3) Passwords; (4) Spells or Invocations for conjuring up the spirit of the dead, or for exorcising demons, or for removing spells on the living; and (5) Cure-charms in formulæ or magic words. Mr. Clodd points out that these classes overlap and intermingle.

Even among such backward people as the Australians, certain of the medicine-men or sorcerers were bards who devoted their poetic faculties to the purposes of enchantment, such as the Bunjil-yenjin of the Kurnai, whose peculiar branch of magic was composing and singing potent love charms and the arrangement of marriages by elopement spells (35, 356, 274).

In few countries was the spoken word more effective than in ancient Ireland; a sorcerer, whether a druid or not, would stand on one foot, with one arm outstretched and with one eye shut, and chant an incantation in a loud voice (37, i. 240). The grand weapon of the Irish poets by which they enforced their demands was the **satire**. A poet could compose a satire that would blight crops, dry up milch-

cows, and raise an ulcerous blister on the face.
A story is told (37, i. 454) of Senchán Torpest,
chief poet of Ireland, who lived in the seventh
century, that once when his dinner was eaten
in his absence by rats, he muttered a satire beginning, 'Rats, though sharp their snouts, are
not powerful in battle,' which killed ten of them
on the spot. Shakespeare, and other Elizabethan
writers, often refer to the belief that Irish bards
could rhyme rats to death. The Irish **geis** or
geas [pronounced gesh or gass], plural *geasa*
[gassa], was the exact equivalent of an ordinary
tabu, but people sometimes put an injunction
on a person in some such form as 'I place you
under heavy *geasa*, which no true champion will
break through, to do so and so.' In this manner,
the witch-lady forces Finn to search for the ring
she had dropped into the lake; and Marbhan put
the arch-poet Senchán Torpest under *geasa* to
obtain a copy of a lost story. When the request
was reasonable or just the abjured person could
not refuse without loss of honour and reputation
and probably in early days personal harm would
accrue if the *geasa* were disregarded. The power
of the *geis* was so strong that when Grania put
Diarmuid under *geasa* of danger and destruction
to elope with her, he was advised by his friends

against his will to agree: Oisin said, 'You are not guilty if the bonds were laid on you,' and Osgar said, 'It is a pitiful man that would break his bonds' (25, 347, 8).

Sympathetic magic bulks largely in the life of backward peoples, not merely in the form of actions to be performed, but also in those to be abstained from. The 'Thou shalt not' is more in evidence than 'Thou shalt.' The prohibitions of savages and barbarians are now spoken of under the general term of **tabu**. Some tabus are rational from our point of view, others seem to us to be utterly irrational, but this does not affect their validity in any way. So much has been written on this subject by divers writers that only one or two examples need be given here. The subject is again referred to on p. 55.

The old Irish tale, the 'Bruiden Dá Derga,' tells of the destruction following the violation of tabus. Conaire, King of Ulster, was put under certain *geasa* by his father, such as: 'Thou shalt not go *desiul* round Tara nor withershins round Bregia,' 'The evil beasts of Cerna must not be hunted by thee,' 'There shall not go before thee three Reds to the house of Red,' and others. But on the way to Dá Derga's Hostel 'They went righthandwise round Tara, and lefthandwise round Bregia, and the evil beasts of Cerna were hunted by him, but he saw it not till the chase had ended.' Then he saw three red men going before him to the house of Red, and Conaire says, 'All my *geasa* have seized me to-night,' and before the next day Conaire and all his host were destroyed in Dá Derga's Hostel (66, xxii.). When Cuchulain was on his way to his last combat he met three hags, daughters of a wizard, all blind of the left eye. They were cooking a dog with poisons and spells on spits of a rowan tree. It was *geis* to Cuchulain to eat at a cooking-hearth, or to eat the flesh of a hound, but the women put him on his honour not to refuse the piece they offered him, so he took it, and all the strength went out of the left hand in which he took the food (66, iii.).

III. TALISMANS AND AMULETS

In the forms of magic we have hitherto considered, something is done by a human being, whether by action, representation, or word, but there is another branch of magic in which the virtue resides intrinsically in certain objects which are variously termed charms, talismans, amulets, or mascots. Those that transmit qualities or are worn for good luck may be termed **talismans**, while the term **amulet** may be restricted with advantage to those charms which are preventive in their action; but the same charm is in some cases employed for both these purposes. These objects are continuously effective without any action on the part of the preparer or wearer, as they possess power in their own right, but this is from very diverse causes.

Certain **stones** from their colour suggest flesh; thus garnets and carnelians are worn in the rough or worked into beads as amulets against skin diseases. Most precious stones are credited with distinctive properties, and some have a reputation for being unlucky, as for example the precious opal. The amethyst, as its name implies, was regarded by the ancient Greeks as a charm against becoming intoxicated; among the ancient Egyptians the amethyst corresponded to the Zodiacal sign of the Goat, and as the goat was an enemy to vines, so the amethyst was a foe to wine. Leland (43, 351) points out that it also 'drives away bad thoughts and confers ripe and happy genius.' Amber beads are carried by people of various races for weak eyes, and it is essential they should be looked through to strengthen the sight (43, 267). The electrical power of attraction of light objects by amber when rubbed was doubtless one cause of its supposed virtue. The several **metals** have their active magical properties. A lump of crude antimony in Italy is very efficacious when the following invocation is pronounced: 'Antimony, who art of zinc and copper! thou most powerful, I keep thee ever by me, that thou mayest banish from me evil people, and bring good luck to me.' Gold is the most genial or luck-bringing, and, as a woman said, 'antimony is stronger than lead, because it consists of three metals, or rather always has in it copper and lead' (43, 373-4).

Colour alone has its magical qualities, hence the frequency of red woollen thread or stuff in counter-charms against the evil eye, as an old saw expresses it: 'Roan tree and red thread, will drive the witches aa wud' (49, 156). For the same reason red coral is so greatly valued. Blue is of equal efficacy, hence the wearing of turquoise by so many Oriental and North African peoples, and blue beads are worn by people for much the same reason, that they suspend them round the necks of donkeys or camels.

When dealing with contagious magic, we saw that many objects are worn, in order that certain qualities of the animals from which they were obtained may be imparted to the wearer. The wild **boar's tusk**, the acquisition of which is greatly desired by the natives of the Papuan Gulf as a mark of bravery, is coveted not so much as a personal ornament, as for the courage, ferocity, and daring which it is supposed to contain and to be capable of imparting to any one who wears it (33, 427). Probably this is the reason why boars' tusks are so much prized all over New Guinea, where they are wrought into 'ornaments,' which are carried in the mouth or worn on the chest when on the war-path. In West Africa the **bones** from the legs of tortoises are much valued as anklets, in order to give the wearers endurance. The lower jaw-bone of the tortoise is worn by certain tribes as a preventive against toothache; in this case the reason would seem to be that as the tortoise has no teeth it cannot suffer from toothache, and thus freedom from toothache can be imparted by that edentulous jaw. The spinal bones of snakes are strung together for a girdle as a cure for backache (3, 237).

Africans, according to Arnot (3, 237), believe largely in preventive measures, and their charms are chiefly of that order. In passing through a country where leopards and lions abound, they carefully provide themselves with **the claws,** teeth, lips, and whiskers of those animals, and hang them around their necks, to secure themselves against being attacked. For the same purpose the point of an elephant's trunk is generally worn by the elephant-hunters.

A large class of talismans consists of models or representations of objects, and the attributes of the original pass on to the symbol. The pig, perhaps on account of its abundant fecundity, was primarily sacred to the earth goddess, whether she was known as Demeter, Ceres, or by any other name. Leland points out (43, 255) that little gold and silver pigs were offered to Ceres, who was pre-eminently a goddess of fertility, and therefore of good luck and all genial influences. For these reasons they were worn by Roman ladies, and 'lucky pigs' are still very common charms, especially in South Germany.

The belief in the evil eye is not only widely spread, but extremely ancient, and in some places is still firmly rooted among the folk. 'Overlooking' may be intentional, but it is believed that many persons, without intention and even against their will, by the glance of their eye, have caused injurious effects; so that, in some cases, mothers would not venture to expose their infants to the look of their own fathers. Plutarch

(18, 13) vouches for this, and admits that envy exerts an evil influence through the eyes, and adds that it is wise to employ charms and antidotes to turn aside these evil glances. A friend of his stated that some even fascinate themselves by their own gaze, and alluded to the story of Eutelidas, who, like Narcissus, fell a victim to the admiration he felt for his own likeness. Women and children seem to have been accounted by all old classical writers as the most liable to injury. Among the Greeks and Romans statues of Nemesis were erected which were adored and invoked to save their worshippers from fascination. In Rome, according to Pliny, special laws were enacted against injury to crops by incantation, excantation, or fascination (18, 15).

'Eat not the bread of him that hath an evil eye' is just as much a maxim to-day as it was in the time of Solomon, and Mr. Elworthy says (18, 107) in Naples, at the appearance of a person having this reputation, a cry of 'Jettatore!' is passed, and even in a crowded street it causes an instantaneous vanishing of everybody—a rush up entries, into shops, or elsewhere. Ever since the establishment of the religious orders, monks have had the special reputation of possessing the fatal influence. The last Pope but one, Pius the

Ninth, was firmly believed to have had the evil eye. A Roman would candidly say: ' Nothing succeeds with anybody or anything when he wishes well to it. When he went to St. Agnese to hold a great festival, down went the floor, and the people were all smashed together. Then he visited the column to the Madonna in the Piazza di Spagna, and blessed it and the workmen; of course, one fell from the scaffold the same day and killed himself' (18, 23, 25).

Domestic animals always have been considered as peculiarly susceptible to this evil influence. Cows are particularly liable to fascination in Scotland, while in England of all animals the pig is most often ' overlooked.' The Turk and the Arab think the same of their horses and camels; above all the Neapolitan cabman of to-day believes in the great danger to his horse from the eye of the *jettatore*.

The commonest of all ancient Egyptian amulets, except the scarab, was ' the Eye of Osiris,' as it is called by us. These mystic eyes were worn equally by the living and the dead as amulets; it being natural, from the associations of homœopathic magic, that representations of the eye itself should have been considered potent amulets against its malign influence. All the peoples

35

round the Mediterranean employed representations of eyes as amulets. In Syria and Cairo necklaces composed of flat glass eyes are sold to the present day, and eye-designs protect the clothes, horse trappings, and many of the objects of daily use of the Moors (72, 211).

Plutarch declares that the objects that are fixed up to ward off witchcraft or fascination derive their efficacy from the fact that they act through the strangeness and ridiculousness of their forms, which fix the mischief-working eye upon themselves.

It was this firm belief, says Elworthy (18, 143), which led to the design of those extremely grotesque figures, of which the ancient Romans were so fond; indeed, anything that was ridiculous or indecent was supposed to be a corrective to the harmful influence of fascination. Amulets which protect against this power are of three classes: (1) Those the object of which was to attract upon themselves the harmful glance (those were necessarily exposed to view); (2) charms worn or carried secretly; and (3) written words of Scripture, Koran, and other sacred writings, or cabalistic figures and formulæ (18, 149).

The crescent moon was a symbol of many deities, Parvati, Devaki, and other Indian goddesses, Isis, Athena or Minerva, Artemis or Diana, and the Madonna. Artemis or Diana was the patroness of domestic animals as well as of the wild creatures of the wood (21, 14); hence we may trace the extreme prevalence of amulets symbolic of their attributes upon horses. The crescent—that is the horned moon—and horns appear to be interchangeable: thus horns, in one form or another, are of all objects the most common as amulets against the evil eye, whether affecting man or beast; so much so, that at last it has come to be fully believed by the Neapolitans, that in default of a horn, in coral or other form, the mere utterance of the word *corno* or *corna* ('horn') is an effectual protection. In Italy, particularly in Naples, the cart harness is literally made up of charms and prophylactics, such as feathers, hair, brightly coloured ribbons, and especially objects of shining brass; of the last the crescent is the most common.

It would take too long to describe all the objects that are employed to counteract the evil eye in Italy alone. The following may be mentioned: fish, snakes, and various other animals, tigers' teeth, keys, a hunchback (*gobbo*). A single pendent horn, whether of coral, shell, or metal is extremely common, as are miniature hands, these frequently have all the digits closed up except the index and little finger, which are fully extended. This is a potent gesture, and a Neapolitan's right hand is almost constantly in that position pointing downwards, just as the hand-charms are made to hang downwards, as a prophylactic against unknown or unsuspected attacks (18, 261). Dr. Westermarck has recently (72, 211) given an illuminating description of the use and representations of the hand against the evil eye in Morocco.

On studying various kinds of talismans and amulets, it at once becomes evident that while some are credited with contagious sympathy, others are mimetic or symbolic, that is homœopathic in their action, while there are many others that owe their efficacy to an intimate relation with a spiritual being of some kind or other, or with a deity. The charms of this third group are to be regarded as **fetishes** so long as the recognition lasts that they are dependent for their virtue upon these extraneous beings; but when this belief is lost the charm becomes a mere talisman or amulet. The change from a fetish to a **luck-object** is constantly taking place owing to the despiritualising effect of increasing civilisation. To take one example, Mr.

TALISMANS AND AMULETS

E. Lovett first drew my attention to the 'luck
bones' that are worn by Whitby, and probably
by other Yorkshire, fishermen, and another friend
subsequently confirmed the fact that these bones
not only bring good fortune but are safeguards
against drowning. The bone in question being
the T-shaped hyoid- or tongue-bone of a sheep,
Mr. Lovett suggested that this bone might have
something to do with Thor's hammer. Later
Professor Boyd Dawkins showed me the identical
bone worn for a similar purpose by Manx fishermen, and it is worthy of note that there were
Scandinavian settlements at both Whitby and the
Isle of Man. I informed Herr E. Friedel of these
facts and inferences, and he discovered (22, 412)
that the men in the Berlin slaughter-yards have
a similar custom, the end of the long arm of the
bone being perforated for a thread that is fastened round the neck of the wearer. On looking
into the archæological evidence he found that in
the early iron age unmistakable representations of
Thor's hammer were worn as charms in Denmark
and Schleswig-Holstein. In those early days
there can be little doubt that the influence of
the god passed into the models of his weapon,
and that these objects partook of the nature of

fetishes, but later the symbols of the god degenerated into luck-objects.

IV. DIVINATION

Men not only attempt to act directly upon nature, but they usually exhibit a keen desire to be guided as to the best course to take when in doubt, difficulty, or danger, and to be forewarned of the future. The practice of **divination** is by no means confined to professional magicians, or even to soothsayers, but any one may employ the accessory means.

Any object may be used in divination: thus in Europe, as in Torres Straits (29, v. 361), a stick may be dropped to indicate a direction to be taken; or coins may be spun or dice thrown. Divination by means of skulls was common in Torres Straits (29, v. 362); in this case the spirit of the dead person was supposed to give the required advice. Haruspication, or divination by means of certain viscera, was largely employed by the Romans, and I have several times seen a pig's liver used in Borneo for the same purpose (28, 336, 354). In these instances the message, as indicated by the state of the particular viscus, was obtained from a deity. Other examples and varieties of divination are given by Tylor (71, i. 123).

V. PUBLIC AND PRIVATE MAGIC

Magic may be employed for public purposes or for private ends. In the former case it is almost invariably for the public weal, in the latter it is most frequently nefarious.

A. Public Magic.

Among some totemic peoples the men of a totem group perform magical ceremonies for the benefit of the community. The best examples of this **communal magic**, as it might be termed, are those described by Messrs. Baldwin Spencer and Gillen (64, 179-183) as practised by the Arunta tribe of Central Australia at the **intichiuma** ceremonies. For example, the headman of a local group of the Emu totem and some other Emu men opened a vein and allowed their blood to stream on a patch of smooth ground, until about three yards were saturated. On the hard surface of the clotted blood the sacred design of the Emu totem was painted with white, yellow, red, and black. It represented certain parts of the emu; two large patches of yellow indicated lumps of fat, of which the natives are very fond, but the greater part represented, by means of circles and circular patches, the eggs in various states of development, some before and some after laying. Various sinuous lines indicated parts of the intestine. Throughout the ceremony the headman was treated with the greatest deference, and no one spoke to him except in a whisper. The sacred wooden slabs (*churinga*) were placed on one side of the painting. In the intervals of a monotonous chant the headman explained the drawing. Three men wore a headdress which represented the long neck and small head of the emu; with a curious gliding movement they approached the spectators, occasionally stopping and moving only their heads imitating the aimless gazing about of the bird.

The witchetty grub *intichiuma* ceremony (64, 170-179) is performed at a special cave, where lies a large block of quartzite surrounded by small rounded stones. The former represents the perfect insect, and the latter its eggs. The headman and his associates tap the large stone and chant songs, the burden of which is an invitation to the insect to lay eggs; the headman strikes each man with one of the small stones, saying, 'You have eaten much food.' Later they go to a large rock which they tap, and invite the animal to come from all directions and lay eggs. After various symbolic ceremonies they enter a long narrow booth made of bushes, which represents the chrysalis case from which the perfect insect emerges, and there they sing of the animal in its various stages and of the sacred stones.

There are many similar ceremonies which the men of a totem group make in order to increase or produce their particular totem; thus, taking the tribe as a whole, the object of these ceremonies is that of increasing the total food supply (64, 315-319). Among the Arunta and Ilpirra only the men of the totem are allowed to be present or to take part in the actual ceremony. During its progress there is always some ceremony, such as that of allowing the blood of young men of the totem to flow over the stone which is associated with the ancestors of the totem. The idea of this is to send the spirits of the animals out of the stone to replenish the stock of the totemic animal. After the ceremony, when, as a consequence, the animal or plant has become abundant, the men of all classes and totems go out and bring supplies into the main camp. No

43

one as yet may eat it. The headman of the totem, in the presence of all in camp, solemnly eats a little and hands the remainder over to the men of the other totems, telling them to eat freely. If the headman did not eat a little he would lose the power of performing *intichiuma* successfully.

In other tribes to the north similar ceremonies exist, but they are less elaborate and sometimes of the simplest description. The headman of the white cockatoo totem group and his son spent the whole of one night 'singing' the cockatoo. In the Wara tribe on the shore of the Gulf of Carpentaria a man of the rain-group goes to a pool, and, taking care that no women or strangers are in sight, bends down over and 'sings' the water; then he takes some up in his hands, drinks it, and spits it out in various directions. After that he throws water all over himself, and after scattering some all round he returns quietly to his camp, and rain is supposed to follow (64, 314). There is very little difference between this act and ordinary individual magic, the essential distinction being that the man in this case makes rain by virtue of rain being his totem, it being a function of human male members of the totem group to increase their totem.

44

PUBLIC MAGIC

When the totemic system falls into decay there seems to be a tendency for the old magical ceremonies which had for their purport the increase of the totem, to be performed by certain families, rather than by groups of men; this appears to be associated with the growth of property in land, so that in time the performance of certain ceremonies is restricted to a single man, who transmits the right to his son, and they alone of the community have this duty. There is nothing to distinguish men with these rights from ordinary sorcerers who practise definite departments of magic.

A very large number of examples of public magical ceremonies, undertaken for the good of the community, have been collected by Dr. Frazer in his *Golden Bough*; of especial interest are those connected with the production of abundant harvests, and the active participation of women in such customs is very significant. I here give an example recently published by Miss Mary Owen (56, 60). The Corn-planting dance of the Musquakie or Fox Indians takes place in April, though the real corn-planting commences about the 1st of May. It is danced by men only; they trot at sunrise along the east side of a cornfield selected by the shaman, going in single file with their rattles and little tambourines or prayer drums, while a young maiden goes into the field and plants a few grains from a perfect ear handed to her by the Honourable Women (women who have borne sons). If the harvest of the year before was scant the dancers may go entirely round the field. Afterwards there is some eating and drinking, but not an elaborate feast. Formerly the real planting of the field followed the ceremonial, and no food was eaten until the women had finished planting. Another old custom was to have the maid who did the planting given a husband, who went with her into the field. Later a prophet had a revelation that this custom should cease. The day is at the present time a favourite one for weddings.

B. Private Magic.

Individuals frequently practise magic for private ends, of which the objects to be attained may be perfectly legitimate or even praiseworthy, but more frequently recourse is had to magical practices for harmful purposes.

Folk remedies for sickness and pains are very frequently of a purely magical character. For example, a common cure for warts is to rub them with a piece of raw meat, which must then be buried; as the meat decays so will the warts disappear: to be effective the meat should be stolen. A woman in Islay was cured of toothache by a man driving a nail into the upper lintel of the kitchen door; he told her to keep it there, and, should it become loose at any time, to tap it a little with a hammer until it had a grip, and he assured her she would be free from toothache. She never again suffered from toothache (49, 158).

Any variety or combination of varieties of sympathetic magic may be employed in the manufacture or practice of **love-charms**; frequently they are fortified by the subtle association of scent. Doubtless certain scents have a direct stimulating effect, but, apart from this, should any scent be definitely worn when young men wish to attract girls, there can be no doubt that the suggestion would tend to act powerfully upon the latter, and that 'girl-medicine,' as I have heard it called, would of itself be potent even if other practices were not employed. I was told by a Torres Straits islander that just as a snake that is in one tree can, by swallowing its spittle, make a bird that is in another tree come to it, so if a man chews a certain medicine and a girl sees him swallowing the infusion in his saliva, she understands what the man means and is constrained to go to him (29, v. 328).

Various instances of **nefarious magic** have been given in the preceding pages. A good example came under my own observation. In Torres Straits there is a vine-like plant that loses its leaves at a certain season of the year, and the stem breaks up into joints, which often bear a striking resemblance to some of the long bones of the human skeleton. This circumstance led magicians to employ these sticks to make human beings into similar dried and shrivelled-up objects. The dry segments of the vine were collected and the magician gave the name of some part of the body to each joint : for example, one would be called an ' arm,' another a ' leg,' and so forth. The magician crouched like a fish-eagle and, imitating the way that a bird tears flesh off bones, threw the segments behind him without looking round. If he left the spot without turning round to look at the sticks the patient would die ; but if he did not wish to proceed to this extremity, he turned and looked at the segments, and subsequently he would return and pick them up and place them together and put ' medicine ' on them, and the patient would recover (29, v. 325).

PRIVATE MAGIC

The following account recently published by Mrs. J. Gunn (26, 98) is so characteristic that I quote it nearly verbatim. In North Australia any one can 'sing magic,' even lubras [women], but of course the wise old magic men do it best. It never fails with them, particularly if they 'sing' and point one of the special 'death-bones' or 'sacred stones' of the tribe. Generally a black fellow goes away quite by himself when he is 'singing magic,' but very occasionally a few men join together, as they did in the case of 'Goggle Eye.' When enough magic has been 'sung' into the bone, it is taken away to the camp, and very secretly pointed at the unconscious victim. The magic spirit of the bone runs into the man who is pointed at, and gradually kills him. Of course the man who has been 'sung' must be told some-how, or he will not get a fright and die. There are many ways of managing this; one very good way is to put the bone where he will be sure to find it, in his dilly-bag, or near his fire, or through the handle of his spear ; but the man who leaves the bone about must, of course, be very careful to destroy his own tracks. 'Goggle Eye,' after he had found the bones lying about, knew exactly what was going to happen to him, and of course it did. His throat got very sore, and he grew so thin and weak that he could hardly stand. A man can be cured by magic men charming the 'bone' away again; but 'Goggle Eye' was old, and, what was worse, he was getting very cross, and too fond of ordering people about, so the black fellows thought it would be the best plan not to cure him, and a few more sneaked away into the bush and 'sang' some more bones, and pointed them at him to make quite sure about his dying. Poor old 'Goggle Eye' suffered dreadfully; no native would help him except his blood-brother, because they were afraid of the curse coming to them. Some said they would like to help, but that if they made 'Goggle Eye's' fire for him, their own would never burn again. Nobody could even carry his food to him. Soon after, at 'fowl sing out,' or cockcrow, he died.

VI. MAGICIANS

Most forms of magic can be performed by anybody provided he knows what to do; but there are specialists in magic, who, by us, are variously termed medicine-men, magicians, sorcerers, wizards, witches, wise women, and the like. Their lore is transmitted orally to their disciples, who may or may not be their own children. Magical powers may be due to the mere accident of birth, as for example in the European belief in the therapeutic gifts of the seventh son of a seventh son. In some cases the sorcerer has to undergo a rigorous training, often being subjected to painful or loathsome ordeals; by these means the weaklings are eliminated, and those who persist have their character and fortitude strengthened, and they gain increased respect from their fellow-men. Further, in Australia and elsewhere, the medicineman is not always a 'doctor'; he may be a 'rain-maker,' 'seer,' or 'spirit-medium,' or may practise some special form of magic.

Usually the sorcerers unite together to form a society, which may attain great influence among backward races. According to Leland (43, 10), 'there is actually in Tuscany a culture or worship of fetishes which are not Catholic, *i.e.* of strange stones and many curious relics. But there is a great deal of mystery and secrecy observed in all this cult. It has its professors; men, but mostly women, who collect charms and spells, and teach them to one another, and hold meetings; that is, there is a kind of college of witches and wizards, which, for many good reasons, eludes observation.' The old faith, as it is termed, is pre-Christian, but not actively anti-Christian.

MAGIC AND FETISHISM

VII. THE PSYCHOLOGY OF MAGICAL PRACTICES

The superficial observer is apt to regard the
medicine-men or sorcerers as cheats who deliber-
ately humbug their neighbours; but it is probable that most of them really believe themselves
to be possessed of occult or supernormal power.
Doubtless they do many things for mere effect,
in order to enhance the respect they desire to
have paid to themselves personally, as well as
to put the subjects or spectators into a proper
frame of mind; but this is precisely what is de-
liberately done by the organisers of all ceremonies
by all peoples. Doubtless, also, many acts are
performed which are intended to impose upon
the credulity of others; but this is a device which
is not unknown among cultured people, as, for
example, the liquefying of the blood of St.
Januarius in Naples. There remain, however, a
large number of phenomena, which are as mysterious to them as they are to the vast majority
of mankind, and many of these are receiving the
attention of psychologists of the present day,
without their significance being understood. Mr.
Podmore (55, 373) is not afraid to say that 'many
of the alleged wonders of witchcraft and of ancient

magic in general, when disentangled from the accretions formed round them by popular myth and superstition, present a marked resemblance to some of the facts recorded ' in his book.

The mental equilibrium of many backward peoples is very unstable, although they may not suffer from the same derangements of the nervous system that affect the more highly civilised peoples. To take an example or two of this **nervous instability**, Castren observed long ago that if the Samoyeds were sitting around inside their skin tents in the evening, and some one crept up and struck the tent, half of them were likely to fall into cataleptic fits. Bogoras (5, 42) refers to the well-known Arctic hysteria which is so widespread among the Yukaghir and Lamut women, and to a less extent among the Chukchee, the Russianised, and even the Russian women. This disease develops chiefly in the form of an uncontrollable desire to repeat in a loud voice each word spoken by somebody else, and to imitate every sudden gesture or action. This is the same nervous disorder as the widely spread *lâtah* of Malaysia, which has been so admirably described by Sir F. A. Swettenham (68, 64).

The far-reaching power of **suggestion** has been perhaps the most potent factor in upholding

53

magical practices, especially when it is **combined with hypnotism**. The hypnotic state, it must be remembered, though ordinarily produced by another, can be self-induced by gazing at an object. There is an overwhelming number of modern instances of bad habits, various diseases, inflammations, local and general pain, insomnia, neurasthenia, psychic paralysis, and psychic hysteria, being cured by suggestion while the patient is in the hypnotic state (31, 607). Conversely pain, inflammations, and other organic changes can be produced through the same means; such is the explanation of the appearance of stigmata on the hands and feet of religious ecstatics, who had induced auto-hypnotism by intently gazing on the Figure on the Cross. The cataleptic and anæsthetic conditions producible by hypnotism are well known all over the world, and have for ages been part of the stock-in-trade of sorcerers, medicine men, or of certain religious enthusiasts.

Suggestion alone, without the aid of hypnotism, can effect wonders, and faith-cures and Christian science are by no means a new thing under the sun, but something very old under new names. Probably every physician has known cases of 'persons who died because they did not want to live or were at least indifferent; and

probably an equal number who materially length-
ened their lives by the mere determination not
to die' (67, 612).

'The psychology of the matter,' writes Marett
(51, 143), 'is up to a certain point simple enough.
Just as the savage is a good actor, throwing himself like a child into his mime, so he is a good
spectator, entering into the spirit of another's
acting, herein again resembling the child, who
can be frightened into fits by the roar of what
he knows to be but a "pretended" lion. Even
if the **make-believe** is more or less make-believe
to the victim, it is hardly less efficacious; for,
dominating, as it tends to do, the field of attention, it racks the emotional system, and, taking
advantage of the relative abeyance of intelligent
thought and will, sets stirring all manner of deep-
lying impulses and automatisms.'

All peoples have prohibitions of certain kinds,
and most have a firm belief that should these
tabus be broken dire consequences will befall the
offender. Occasionally the punishment is effected
by the social executive, through representatives
of secret societies or by other means; but usually
it is left in the hands, so to speak, of the out-
raged spiritual powers, and so strong is this belief that it drees its own weird. For example,

MAGIC AND FETISHISM

Father Merolla (54, xvi. 238) tells of a young
Congo negro who, being on a journey, lodged at
a friend's house; the latter got a wild hen for his
breakfast, and the young man asked if it were
a wild hen. His host replied 'No.' Then he fell
on heartily, and afterwards proceeded on his
journey. After four years these two met together
again, and his old friend asked him 'If he would
eat a wild hen,' to which he answered that it was
tabooed to him. 'Hereat the host began immediately to laugh, inquiring of him, "What made
him refuse it now, when he had eaten one at his
able about four years ago?" At the hearing
of this the negro immediately fell a-trembling,
and suffered himself to be so far possessed with
the effects of imagination that he died in less
than twenty-four hours after.' Armit (2, 459)
relates that an Australian died of fright within a
fortnight after he had discovered his sick wife
had lain upon his blanket. Nowhere is the power
of taboo greater than among the Polynesians.
And examples of its potency in procuring its
own fulfilment in the Heroic Age of Ireland
have already been given (p. 29).

No wonder then that belief in the magical
powers of sorcerers can cause the same effects.
Messrs. Spencer and Gillen (64, 537) state that

the Australian natives believe that any bone, stick, spear, etc., which has been 'sung' is supposed to be endowed with what the natives call *Arungquiltha,* that is, magical poisonous properties, and any native who believes that he has been struck by, say, a charmed spear, is almost sure to die, whether the wound be slight or severe, unless he be saved by the counter magic of a medicine-man. He simply lies down, refuses food, and pines away. Actual instances are given of men with slight wounds dying in a few days from this belief.

There can be no doubt that magical practices can act by **suggestion** through **fear** and **fascination** upon human victims who are aware of their occurrence, and it is probable that in most cases the victim is made aware of such practices as in the instance given on p. 49. Also there is every reason to believe that all backward peoples, including the sorcerers themselves, believe in the power of magic. Casalis (10, 275) gives an instructive instance in point. A chief of the Basutos once held forth in his presence on the matter of sorcery: he said, 'Sorcery only exists in the mouths of those who speak of it. It is no more in the power of man to kill his fellow by the mere effect of his will, than it would be to raise him from the dead. This is my opinion. Nevertheless, you sorcerers who hear me speak, use moderation.'

Probably more widely spread than is usually accepted is the belief of some backward peoples, and therefore of their magicians, in a spiritual force that accomplishes their desires; such, for example, as the **mana** of the Melanesians. 'The Melanesian mind,' writes Dr. Codrington (12, 118), 'is entirely possessed by the belief in a supernatural power or influence, called almost universally *mana*. This is what works to effect everything which is beyond the ordinary power of man, outside the common processes of nature; it is present in the atmosphere of life, attaches itself to persons and to things, and is manifested by results which can only be ascribed to its operation. When one has got it he can use it and direct it, but its force may break forth at some new point; the presence of it is ascertained by proof. A man comes by chance upon a stone which takes his fancy; its shape is singular, it is like something, it is certainly not a common stone, there must be *mana* in it. So he argues with himself, and he puts it to the proof; he lays it at the root of a tree to the fruit of which it has a certain resemblance, or he buries it in the ground when he plants a garden; an abundant crop on the tree or in the garden shows that he is right, the stone is *mana*, has that power in it. Having that power, it is a vehicle to convey *mana* to other stones. In the same way certain forms of words, generally in the form of a song, have power for certain purposes; a charm of words is called *mana*. But this power, though itself impersonal, is always connected with some person who directs it; all spirits have it, ghosts generally, some men. If a stone is found to have a supernatural power it is because a spirit has associated itself with it. A dead man's bone has with it *mana*, because the ghost is with the bone; a man may have so close a connection with a spirit or ghost that he has *mana* in himself also, and can so direct it as to effect what he desires. All conspicuous success is a proof that a man has *mana* ; his influence depends on the impression made on the people's mind that he has it.' If a man has been successful in fighting, it is not through his own qualities, but ' he has certainly got the *mana* of some deceased warrior to empower him, conveyed in an amulet of a stone round his neck, or a tuft of leaves in his belt, in a tooth hung upon the finger of his bow hand, or in the form of words with which he brings supernatural assistance to his side.'

The Omaha (19) believe that a man's own will can act directly on his fellows by singing certain songs; this act is called *wazhin-dhedhe*, that is 'directive energy, to send'; the Omaha term 'signifies to send forth one's thought and **will power** toward another in order to supplement his strength, and thereby affect his action,' or, as we should term it, **telepathy.** By an appeal to *Wakanda* (that is 'immanent life manifest in all things,' or the 'hidden and mysterious power which brings to pass'), in the rite of vision, the man's powers could be supplemented by the co-operation of the elements and of animals.

The innate spirituality of the savage appears to be largely ignored by students, who usually dub the magic worker as a conscious cheat and humbug, whereas it seems to be more correct to regard him as dealing with material objects mainly as endowed with life (**Animism**; 50, 171), or as the vehicles of spiritual or supernatural power, and by means of such objects or by the shafts of speech he can effectively project his will.

If then, as Mr. Marett points out (51, 150), the occult projectiveness of the magical act is naturally and almost inevitably interpreted as an exertion of will that somehow finds its way to another will and dominates it, the spell or uttered 'must' will tend to embody the very life and soul of the affair. Nothing finds its way home to another's mind more sharply. It is the very type of a spiritual projectile.

In many examples of magical procedure the magician appears to act directly upon nature, and seeks to enforce the action of his will by the power of the spoken word or spell. In other cases he obtains power from energy derived from something outside of himself; for example, the shaman of Siberia may be possessed by a spirit, or the magician may even be possessed by a god. Thus by insensible stages do we arrive at actions that may better be described as religious or theurgic than as magical. Numerous examples of transition stages are given by Mr. W. W. Skeat (63). The god-inspired magician may become an actual deity, for many royal magicians, who are more especially rain-makers, are regarded, as Dr. Frazer has recently pointed out, as incarnate gods in Africa and elsewhere (21). Concurrently with ideas of personification and progressive deification the **spell evolves into prayer.** On the other hand, power may be obtained over deities by practices that are essentially magical, as, for

example, by uttering the ineffable name, or by
spells and incantations, and these may at the
same time be associated with prayer, or the
prayer itself may degenerate into a spell.

However it may be with human beings, few
culture-folk will admit that sorcerers can effect
the ordinary phenomena of nature, and in this
respect, at all events, they should soon become
discredited. On one occasion in Murray Island,
Torres Straits, a native showed me two stones
in a recess on the foreshore which were pointed
at by men holding certain leaves which were
left there. A 'big wind' would immediately
arise which lasted until the plants were removed.
This *zogo* was employed only in the season of
the South-east trade wind. On my asking
whether the ceremony was done in the North-
west monsoon, my informant said emphatically,
'Can't do it in North-west.' That is, the charm
is performed only at that season of the year
when the required result is possible—indeed,
when it is of normal occurrence (28, 60; 29,
vi.) In this, as in other cases, I found that
the impossible was never attempted. A rain
charm would not be made when there was no
expectation of rain coming, or a south-east wind
be raised during the wrong season. Probably

this is the experience of others elsewhere, and thus it is not remarkable if the desired result frequently follows the performance of the charming.

A loophole is generally provided in case of failure. Either some irregularity or mistake occurred in the performance of the charm, or another sorcerer was performing contrary magic which proved of greater potency.

FETISHISM

I. DEFINITION

THE word Fetishism has been so misused of late
that ethnologists are apt to view it askance and
hesitate to employ it in religious classifications.
It has been stretched to such an extent in various
directions that it has lost the definition and pre-
cision necessary for a scientific term. Starting
from a humble origin, referring in its native land
(Portugal) to the charms and amulets worn 'for
luck,' and to relics of saints, 'fetish' grew to such
amazing proportions when transplanted to West
African soil, that at last there was nothing connected with West African religion to which it was
not applied. De Brosses introduced Fétichisme
as a general descriptive term (8), supposing
the word to be connected with *chose fée, fatum*.
Comte[1] employed it to describe the universal
religious tendency to which Dr. Tylor has

[1] *Philosophie Positive.*

64

given the name of Animism (71, chaps. xi.-xvii.).
Bastholm claimed 'everything produced by nature
or art, which receives divine honour, including
the sun, moon, earth, air, fire, water, with rivers,
trees, stones, images and animals, considered as
objects of divine worship, as Fetishism;[1] and
Lippert (46) defines Fetishism as 'a belief in the
souls of the departed coming to dwell in any
thing that is tangible or visible in heaven or
earth.'

Although Miss Kingsley (39, 139) expresses
regret that the word Fetish 'is getting very
loosely used in England,' she scarcely helps forward the work of distinction and arrangement
when a few lines further on she announces ' When
I say Fetish, or Ju Ju, I mean the religion of the
natives of West Africa.' Subsequently she over-
stepped her own definition, describing the secret
societies as 'pure fetish' (41, 139), although they
'are not essentially religious,' but 'are mainly
judicial.'

The Rev. R. H. Nassau perpetuates this vague
use of the word, grouping under the name of
Fetishism all native customs even remotely connected, as everything is in West Africa, with religious or magical beliefs, until the ejaculation

[1] *Historische Nachrichten zur Kenntniss der Menschen.*

uttered when one sneezes or stumbles receives the sounding title, 'fetish prayer' (53, 97).

These 'lumpings' are all the more to be regretted since Miss Kingsley and the Rev. R. H. Nassau are among the chief authorities on West African Fetishism in its most characteristic forms, and a clear definition of the use of the word, with a rigid adherence to its proper meaning, would have done great service in preventing many misconceptions.

The meaning of any word depends upon its definition, and it may be defined in three ways: 1. etymologically; 2. historically; 3. dogmatically.

1. The word fetish is derived through the Portuguese *feitiço* from the Latin *facticius— facere*=to do. This shows the original conception at the root of the word.

2. The historical definition shows the growth or evolution of the meaning of the word, starting from its original conception. Dr. Tylor has pointed out how magic has appropriated to itself the derivatives of 'to do,' such as *feitiço* in Portuguese, *fattura* in Italian, *faiture* in Old French, and many more, thus claiming to be 'doing' *par excellence* (70, 135). This tendency is already noticeable even in classical

times ('*potens et factiosus*,' possessed of power and influence, Auct. *Her.* 2, 26, 40), and is well marked in Plautus, who uses various derivatives of *facere* to mean 'powerful' or 'influential,' especially with reference to influence due to family connection or to riches (*factiones, Aul.* ii. i. 45; *factiosus*, ib. ii. ii. 50; *factio, Cist.* ii. i. 17, etc.). From this sense of **potent politically**, later Latin developed the meaning of **potent magically**, as seen in *facturari*, to bewitch, *factura*, witchcraft, from which latter is descended the Old French *faiture*, witchcraft, and perhaps our slang word 'fake.' **Fetish** as derived from the passive form *facticius*, meaning made by art, artificial, was probably first applied to images, idols or amulets made by hand, and later included **all objects possessing magical potency,** *i.e.* bewitched or 'faked.' [1]

3. The dogmatic definition of a word is the meaning attached to it by individuals of authority.

Fetishism is defined as 'the worship of inanimate objects,' the worship of stocks and stones, 'the religious worship of material objects' (61, 61), 'tangible and inanimate objects worshipped

---

[1] For the references to the suggestive use of the word by **Plautus,** I am indebted to Miss Rachel White of Newnham College.

for themselves alone' (15, 196), and a fetish is defined as 'differing from an idol in that it is worshipped in its own character, not as the symbol, image, or occasional residence of a deity' (*New English Dictionary*, Oxford, Clarendon Press, 1901).

The account of the native of Fida given by Bosman (54, xvi. 493) is often quoted as the classic example of fetishism :—

'I once asked a negro with whom I could talk very freely . . . how they celebrated their divine worship, and what number of gods they had ; he, laughing, answered that I had puzzled him ; and assured me that nobody in the whole country could give me an exact account of it. "For, as for my own part, I have a very large number of gods, and doubt not but that others have as many." "For any of us being resolved to undertake anything of importance, we first of all search out a god to prosper our designed undertaking ; and going out of doors with the design, take the first creature that presents itself to our eyes, whether dog, cat, or the most contemptible creature in the world for our god : or perhaps instead of that, any inanimate that falls in our way, whether a stone, a piece of wood, or anything else of the same nature. This new-chosen god is immediately presented with an offering, which is accompanied by a solemn vow, that if it pleaseth him to prosper our undertakings, for the future we will always worship and esteem him as a god. If our design prove successful, we have discovered a new and assisting god, which is daily presented with a fresh offering; but if the contrary happen, the new god is rejected as a useless tool, and consequently returns to his primitive estate." "We make and break our gods daily, and consequently are the masters and inventors of what we sacrifice to." '

Bosman goes on to say :—

'I was very well pleased to hear the negro talk in this manner concerning his country gods; but, having conversed with him for some time, I observed that he ridiculed his own country gods, for, having lived amongst the French, whose language he perfectly understood and spoke, he had amongst them imbibed the principles of the Christian religion, and somewhat towards a just notion of the true God and how he is to be worshipped, . . . wherefore he no further concerned himself with the gods of the country than as engaged to it for quietness' sake, or to make his friends easy.'

A sceptic is scarcely likely to give a sympathetic report of a religion he has discarded, and Bosman's negro is no exception to the rule. He describes the outward tangible aspect of fetishism, but ignores its spiritual interpretation, and the dogmatic definitions above follow in the same path of error.

Fetishism and the fetish, as thus defined, do

not exist, except in 'incomplete observations'; they certainly are nowhere to be found in West Africa, the typical land of fetishism.

'Every native with whom I have conversed on the subject,' writes Ellis, 'has laughed at the possibility of it being supposed that he could worship or offer sacrifice to some such object as a stone, which of itself it would be perfectly obvious to his senses was a stone only and nothing more' (15, 192). So the Maori *waka-pakoko* were only thought to possess virtue or peculiar sanctity from the presence of the god they represented when dressed up for worship; at other times they were regarded only as bits of ordinary wood (69, 212), and Brinton affirms that 'nowhere in the world did man ever worship a stick or a stone as such' (6, 131).

All cases of Fetishism, when examined, show that the worship is paid to an intangible power or spirit incorporated in some visible form, and that the fetish is merely the link between the worshipper and the object of his worship. Any definition therefore which takes no account of the spiritual force behind the material object is seen to be incomplete and superficial, as it ignores the essential conception of the worship.

DEFINITION OF FETISHISM

Dr. Tylor enlarges the scope of the word, classing Fetishism as a subordinate department of Animism, and defining it as the doctrine of spirits embodied in, or conveying influence through, certain material objects. He includes in it the worship of stocks and stones, 'and thence it passes by an imperceptible gradation into idolatry' (71, ii. 144).

It is these imperceptible gradations which blur all the outlines of the rigid systematist, and make an exclusive classification impossible. Encouragement is found in the reflection that exclusive classifications are almost unknown to science, and, where met with, are generally due to ignorance, waiting for greater knowledge or further research to provide the intermediate links which everywhere blend class with class, species with species. But when the group is studied in its area of characterisation, certain features stand prominently forward, and by a study of these the essential characteristics of the whole class can be determined.

II. ESSENTIAL CHARACTERS OF
FETISHISM

The characteristic features of fetishism, and particularly of West African fetishism, are as follows :—

The fetish may consist of any object whatsoever, but the object chosen is generally either a wonderful ornament or curiosity, a symbolic charm with sympathetic properties, or a sign or token representing an ideal notion or being. It is credited with mysterious power, owing to its being, temporarily or permanently, the vessel or habitation, vehicle for communication, or instrument of some unseen power or spirit, which is conceived to possess personality and will, and ability to see, hear, understand, and act. It may act by the will or force of its own power or spirit, or by force of a foreign power entering it or acting on it from without, and the material object and the power or spirit may be dissociated. It is worshipped, prayed to, sacrificed to, talked with, and petted or ill-treated with regard to its past or future behaviour. In its most characteristic form a fetish must be consecrated by a priest.

1. **A fetish may be any object whatsoever,** but there is always a reason for its choice.

The simplest reason is **that it attracts atten-**

tion (61, 61) (71, ii. 145), and anything that
attracts attention at once acquires an exaggerated
value, and appeals to that natural instinct of
human nature, found also among some birds and
animals, the love for collecting.

' In the love of abnormal curiosities there shows
itself a craving for the marvellous, an endeavour
to get free from the tedious sense of law and
uniformity in nature' (71, ii. 145).

So the fetish consists of a queer-shaped stone, a
bright bead, a stick, parrots' feathers, a root, claw,
seed, bone, or any curious or conspicuous object.

In Benin they take everything which seems
extraordinary in nature for a god, and make offerings to him, and each is his own priest, in order
to worship his gods in what manner pleases him
best (54, xvi. 530).

Or the object may have attracted attention
by its behaviour.

A visitor to a fetish hut took up a stone about as
big as a hen's egg, and its owner told its history.
' He was once going out on important business,
but crossing the threshold he trod on this stone
and hurt himself. Ha, ha! thought he, art thou
here? So he took the stone, and it helped him
through his undertaking for days ' (71, ii. 158).

Sometimes the object to be chosen is revealed

to a man in a dream, as among the natives of
the Gold Coast, where a dead relation will return
to direct a man to go to a certain spot and
there select a certain stone, or piece of a tree,
which he is to bring home with him, and guard and
reverence as the habitation of a protecting deity
(15, 90).

This connects the fetish with the guardian spirits
of the North American Indians, which appear
to young men in dreams, or visions, after prayer
and fasting. The vision generally takes the form
of some tangible object, often an animal, a portion
of which is preserved by the man as his most
precious possession, and if not, some concrete
form is taken to represent the subject of the
vision. A guardian spirit differs, however, from
a fetish, in that it is a life-long possession, some
men are not privileged to obtain one, and no man
could possess more than one; while any man
could obtain a fetish, and could discard one and
adopt another if it proved to be unavailing.

2. It consists of a symbolic charm with sympathetic properties. 'There is a relation between
the selected substances and the object to be obtained: to give the possessor bravery or strength,
some part of a leopard or an elephant; to give
cunning, some part of a gazelle; to give wisdom,

some part of a human brain; to give courage, some part of a heart; to give influence, some part of an eye,' etc. etc. 'These substances are supposed to lure some spirit (being in some way pleasing to it) which thenceforward is satisfied to reside in them and to aid the possessor in the accomplishment of some specific wish' (53, 82).

For convenience of carriage these substances are put into snail-shells, nut-shells, or the small horns of gazelles, or of goats, and the whole then forms the fetish.

Bosman describes the way in which a fetish, consisting of a pipe filled with various substances, was generally made on the Guinea Coast in 1705.

'They have a great wooden pipe filled with earth, oil, blood, bones of dead men and beasts, feathers, hair, and to be short, all sorts of excrementitious and filthy trash, which they do not endeavour to mould into any shape, but lay it in a confused heap in the pipe' (54, xvi. 398).

'Human eyeballs, particularly of white men, are a great charm. This, I fancy, is to secure the man "that lives in your eyes" for the service of the village' (40, 305).

Sometimes there is a tangible connection between the object chosen for the fetish and the spirit occupying it. Thus among the Gold Coast natives the object which is entered by the subordinate spirit of Sasabonsum must be taken from the habitat of a Sasabonsum, from a place, that is, which is marked with red earth, where the red earth marks the blood of the victim of a Sasabonsum (15, 109),

3. It may consist of **a sign or token representing an ideal notion or being**, and here it is difficult to draw any distinction between fetishism and idolatry, 'for a small line and a few streaks of colour may change a fetish into an idol' (61, 77). Certainly the lower forms of idolatry present the aspect of fetishism, but the true fetish is not shaped to resemble the spirit it represents, and the true idol is only the symbol, not the vessel, vehicle, or instrument of deity. At the same time, an image may be worshipped as a fetish, and regarded as a material body provided for a spirit; or a fetish, being regarded merely as the symbol or representative of a spirit, seems to develop the earliest form of idolatry (71, ii. 169). The distinction lies in the attitude of mind in which the objects are worshipped, and no objective differentiation is possible, for the object will be a fetish for one worshipper and a pure symbol of a spirit to another.

Stone worship is often pure fetishism, the stone

being regarded as the tangible sign or token of a spirit or power to which worship is addressed. But it advances beyond the limits of fetishism if a general spirit, or a god of a community, while worshipped in the form of a stone, is also believed to animate other objects. The animating force of a fetish must be individual, and cannot animate more than one object at a time. When the spirits of the *suhman* charms (15, 99) are considered to be individual spirits dependent upon Sasabonsum they are fetishes; if the spirit of Sasabonsum were supposed to animate all the *suhman* charms they could not properly be called fetishes.

4. A fetish is **credited with mysterious powers owing to its being the habitation, temporary or permanent, of a spiritual being.**

This sounds like a definition of the principle of animism, and so it may be, for fetishism is animism, seen, as it were, from the other end and seen in detail. Animism sees all things animated by spirits; fetishism sees a spirit incorporated in an individual object.

But there is this distinction, that the spirit which is believed to occupy the fetish is a different conception from the spirit of the animistic theory; it is not the soul or vital power belonging to the

MAGIC AND FETISHISM

object, and inherent in it, from which the virtue is derived, but a spirit or power attracted to and incorporated in it, while separable from it. The spirit of the fetish is also distinct from a god, as it can animate one object only, while a god can manifest his power in various forms.

Thus in Bosman's account of the Benin fetish quoted above, he talks of 'the pipe where the idol is lodged,' that is the material habitation into which the spirit has been lured by some means of attraction. Miss Kingsley, describing a fetish or *juju*, says 'it is not a doll or toy, and has far more affinity to the image of a saint, inasmuch as it is not venerated for itself, or treasured because of its prettiness, but only because it is the residence, or the occasional haunt, of a spirit' (40, 287).

The material objects which form the tutelary deities or *Bohsŭm* of the natives of the Gold Coast are not symbols of gods which usually reside elsewhere; each is the actual receptacle or ordinary abiding-place of an indwelling god. One may be a wooden figure, another a stone, a third a covered calabash or an earthen pot, containing a mixture of blood and earth (15, 80).

The best example of this class is provided by the *suhman.*

FETISHISM

The man who wants a *suhman* takes some
objects, it may be a rudely cut wooden image,
or a stone, a root of a plant, or some red earth
placed in a pan, and then he calls on a spirit
of Sasabonsum ('a genus of deities, every mem-
ber of which possesses identical characteristics')
to enter the object prepared, promising it offerings and worship. If a spirit consents to take
up its residence in the object a low hissing sound
is heard, and the *suhman* is complete. It receives a small portion of the daily food of its
owner, and is treated with reverence, and mainly
used to bring evil on some one else (15, 100-
101).

5. Sometimes the fetish is merely **the vehicle
or means by which the spirit communicates** with
his worshippers, and only acquires a temporary
personality when thus inspired. This is the
character of the New Zealand fetishes, *wakapa-
koko*, or images.

'A small image was used about 18 inches
long, resembling a peg, with a carved head. The
priest first bandaged a fillet of red parrot feathers
under the god's chin, which was called his *pahau*
or beard; when this was done it was taken possession of by the *atua*, whose spirit entered it; the
priest then either held it in the hand and

vibrated it in the air, whilst the powerful *karakia* (charm, prayer) was repeated, or he tied a piece of string, formed of the centre of a flax leaf, round the neck of the image and stuck it in the ground: he sat at a little distance from it, holding the string in his hand, and gave the god a jerk to arrest his attention' (69, 182).

These Maori fetishes 'were only thought to possess virtue or peculiar sanctity from the presence of the god they represent when dressed up, at other times they were regarded as bits of ordinary wood' (69, 212). The use of the words 'image' and 'god' seem to place this ceremony on a higher plane than fetishism, but the 'god' is generally the spirit of an ancestor, and the 'image' is less a portrait of a worshipped deity than an expression of the Maori genius for wood-carving.

6. While the conception of the fetish as the vehicle of communication between spirit and worshipper raises fetishism to a higher plane in religious evolution, the conception of the fetish **as an instrument by which the spirit acts** lowers it to a stage which is not necessarily religious at all, to a stage where the fetish is often regarded merely in the light of a charm or an amulet.

FETISHISM

This is the lowest and the commonest form of fetishism; it may practically be said to be universal.

Bosman relates that the word Fetiche is chiefly used in a religious sense, or at least is derived from thence, but 'all things made in honour of these false gods, never so mean, are called Fetiche.'

These material charms are so common that by the universality of their use, and the prominence given to them everywhere, in houses and on the person, they almost monopolise the religious thought of the Bantu negro, subordinating other acknowledged points of his theology, dominating his almost entire religious interest, and giving the departmental word 'fetich' such overwhelming regard that it has furnished the name distinctive of the native African religious system (53, 80). 'The new-born infant has a health-knot tied about his neck, wrists, or loins, and down to the day of oldest age every one keeps on multiplying or renewing or altering these life talismans' (53, 85).

It is interesting to find this form of fetish charm described by Bosman at the beginning of the eighteenth century.

'The child is no sooner born than the priest

(here called Fetichee or Confoe) is sent for, who binds a parcel of ropes and coral and other trash about the head, body, arms, and legs of the infant; after which he exorcises, according to their accustomed manner, by which they believe it is armed against all sickness and ill accidents, and doubtless this is as effectual as if done by the Pope himself' (54, xvi. 388).

Father Merolla, a still earlier traveller, mentions these charms from the Congo district (1682).

'The fourth abuse is that whilst their children are young these people bind them about with certain superstitious cords made by the wizards, who likewise teach them to utter a kind of spell while they are binding them. They also at the same time hang about them bones and teeth of divers animals, being preservatives, as they say, against the power of any disease. Likewise there are some mothers so foolish that they will hang Agnus Deis, medals, and relicks to the aforesaid cords' (54, xvi. 237). 'To remedy these disorders, we have thought proper to issue forth the following ordinances: That all mothers should make the cords they bound their infants with of palm leaves that had been consecrated on Palm Sunday; moreover guard them well with other such relicks as we are accustomed to make use of at the time of baptism' (54 xvi. 239).

These fetish charms may be worshipped and regarded as anthropopathic, when they are true fetishes, or they may be merely 'lucky' with no religious regard or spiritual interpretation, or they may be anything between the two extremes.

7. Just as the human body and soul form one individual, so the material object and its occupying spirit or power form one individual, more vague perhaps, but still with many attributes distinctively human. It possesses **personality and will**, it has also many human characters. It possesses most of the human passions, anger, revenge, also generosity and gratitude; it is within reach of influence and may be benevolent, hence to be deprecated and placated, and its aid enlisted (53, 62).

The objects used as fetishes by the Ainu, sticks, skulls of animals, claws, paws, mistletoe, stones, etc., are all looked upon as animate, with a distinct life of their own, with power to protect their worshippers in time of danger, heal them when sick, and bless them with general prosperity (4, 375-6).

In this characteristic, in the possession of personality and will, in its material and spiritual duality, a fetish differs from a charm or an amulet as from an idol; it is always 'anthropopathic' (61, 61).

8. The fetish may **act by will or force of its own proper spirit,** or **by force of a foreign spirit, entering or acting on it from without.**

'Beyond the regularly recognised habitats of the spirits, that may be called natural to them, any other location may be acquired by them temporarily, for longer or shorter periods' (53, 62).

When the fetish acts by force of its own proper spirit, it is something more than mere Animism (*v.* above, p. 77). It does not become a fetish by applying the general belief in souls to a special object, but by a process which has been divided by Schultze into four stages (62, 215-223) :—

1. The value which an uncultured man attributes to any object is often exaggerated, especially if the object is in any way conspicuous, unusual, or mysterious.

2. He attributes to it an anthropopathic nature, believing that all natural objects are like man, with human characteristics.

3. By the causal connection of ideas he associ-

ates the object with auspicious or inauspicious events, which he believes it to influence.

4. A belief in its power leads him to reverence it, and to attempt to conciliate and propitiate the power by worship.

As an example, the anchor cast up on the beach at the mouth of the river Keissi (45) may be cited :—

1. The anchor was an unusual object, and was therefore credited with an exaggerated value and regarded with great interest.

2. It was believed to possess a life of its own, a soul or spirit, somewhat analogous to man's.

3. A Kaffir broke off a piece of the anchor, and he soon afterwards died. The two events were associated with one another, and the breaking of the anchor was believed to have caused the death.

4. The power of the anchor-spirit was thus established, and the natives worshipped it in fear and hope.

Thus the fetish was evolved.

But more commonly a spirit is attracted to the object from without, as in the case of the *suhman* of the Gold Coast, where the spirit of the Sasabonsum is invited into the stone or other object prepared for it, or as in the most usual type of West African fetish, where the wandering spirit becomes localised in an object by means of the ceremonies and conjurings of the Uganga or magic doctor (53, 81).

The distinction between the different powers animating the fetish are clearly distinguishable on the Gold Coast (16, 275). The Tshi believe that everything in nature is animated; that everything not made with hands has an indwelling spirit, possessing powers beneficial or prejudicial to man, according to whether it is propitiated or neglected; so the more dangerous spirits, those of rivers, mountains, rocks, and shoals are worshipped. Later on an image is made of the nature-god, from material from his habitat, and it is brought to a place more convenient for the worshippers, and forms their tutelary deity. Gradually his origin is forgotten, and the nature-god becomes a fetish.

But besides these 'nature-gods' there are 'ghost-gods.' The fetish may be animated by a 'ghost-god,' for the power of dead men lives on in their ghosts; sacrifices are made to them, and ghost-gods also develop into tutelary deities. Perhaps ancestor-worship and Fetishism may be more intimately related than is generally acknowledged (16, 280). The Melanesians believe that the souls of the dead act through bones; while the independent spirits choose stones as their mediums (6, 131).

9. In the popular view of Fetishism the material object was worshipped in its own character, but one of the fundamental conceptions of the West African fetish is that **the spirit and the material object can be dissociated,** and that, although the spirit is temporarily incorporated in the fetish, yet the two are no more inseparable than man's soul and body. The conception of the duality of everything lies at the root of all the West African beliefs. 'Everything that he knows by means of his senses he regards as a two-fold entity—part spirit, part not spirit, or, as we should say, matter; the connection of a certain spirit with a certain mass of matter, he holds, is not permanent. He will point out to you a lightning-struck tree, and tell you its spirit has been broken; he will tell you, when the cooking-pot has been broken, that it has lost its spirit; if his weapon fails, it is because some one has stolen, or made its spirit sick by witchcraft. In every action of his life he shows you how much he lives with a great powerful spirit world around him' (39, 141).

MAGIC AND FETISHISM

When the spirit is 'dead' the fetish has no further value, 'the little thing you kept the spirit in is no more use now, and only fit to sell to a white man as "a big curio"!' (40, 304-5). But occasionally sanctity still clings to the former dwelling of the spirit, and it is used as a charm, though no longer worshipped as a fetish.

The *Mirrone*, a tree worshipped in the Congo region, was the tutelar god of the dwelling, and the owners placed calabashes full of palm-tree wine at the foot of the tree for the spirit to drink, 'nor do they dare to tread upon its leaves any more than we would on the holy cross.' But if it were damaged in any way, they no longer worshipped it, but they stripped off the bark or rind, which was made into petticoats for the women, to act as protecting charms (54, xvi. 236). Owing to the possibility of the spirit leaving the fetish, it has to be tested, to see whether it really contains an indwelling spirit or no, and the natives of the Gold Coast put their Bohsum in the fire as a probation. If the fire injures it in the very least degree, it is not a true Bohsum, there is no indwelling spirit (15, 92).

Sometimes the spirit is forcibly ejected from his dwelling-place for a particular purpose. Soon after Sir Richard Burton had arrived at Dahomé, 'a fetish youth made his appearance in the evening, knelt down before the domestic altar, broke some of the images, and went away declaring that he had called out the fetishes, and that I might after the *evocatio deorum* do my worst' (9, i. 299).

10. The fetish is **worshipped, prayed to, sacrificed to, and talked with,** as a sentient and willing personification of the spirit or power. Examples of sacrifices and prayers and worship offered to the fetishes are found in all parts, and many instances have already been quoted.

Offerings of food and drink are placed before them daily, and sometimes a cock is sacrificed; occasionally, if the worshippers are rich, a sheep is killed, 'which they offer up to the gods in words alone, for they immediately fall upon it and tear it to pieces with their fingers' (54, xvi. 400).

The personal interest of the fetishes in the affairs of their worshippers is seen in the ceremonies connected with the death and burial of the Fiote. 'When all are assembled, the elder addresses the two family fetishes held by two of the family. Pointing and shaking his hand at them, he tells them how the deceased died, and all the family has done to settle the matter; he tells them how they have allowed the father to be taken, and prays them to protect the rest of the family; and when he has finished his address the two who hold the fetishes pick up a little earth and throw it on the heads of the fetishes, then, lifting them up, rub their heads in the earth in front of them ' (13, 135).

11. The fetish is petted or ill-treated with regard to its past or future behaviour. The spirit is invited to enter the *suhman* charm prepared for it by promises of offerings and food (16, 100), and special offerings are made before embarking on any great enterprise.

But when conciliation fails, the owner sometimes has resort to force, though Colonel Ellis states that in all his experience of the natives of the Gold Coast he has never seen or heard of any coercion of a fetish by the natives, and that the idea of coercion is entirely foreign to their minds (15, 194). The Kafirs appear to be harsher in their methods.

' The Caffres play at a game of chance before their idols, and, should chance be against them, kick and box their idols; but if, after this correction, on pursuing their experiments they should continue unsuccessful, they burn the hands and feet of them in the fire; should ill fortune still

attend them, they cast the idols on the ground,
tread them under foot, dash them about with
such force as to break them to pieces. Some,
indeed, who show greater veneration for the
images, content themselves with fettering and
binding them until they have obtained their end;
but should this not take place as early as their
impatience looks for, they fasten them to a cord
and gradually let them down into the water, even
to the bottom, thus trusting to force them to be
propitious; if after this good fortune should not
follow, the idols are then withdrawn from the
water, the patience of even the milder Caffres
becomes exhausted, and the images are subjected
to the grossest indignations ' (54, xvi. 696).

The negro in Guinea beats his fetish if his
wishes are frustrated, and hides it in his waist-
cloth when he is about to do something of which
he is ashamed (38, 91).

III. FETISHISM AS A FORM OF RELIGIOUS WORSHIP

Fetishism is a stage of religious development
associated with a low grade of consciousness and
of civilisation, and it forms a basis from which
many other modes of religious thought have

developed, so that it is difficult to point out where fetishism ends and nature-worship, ancestor-worship, totemism, polytheism, and idolatry begin, or to distinguish between a fetish, an idol, and a deity.

It includes conceptions which are purely magical, coercion of the supernatural by means of natural objects; and it also includes conceptions which persist into higher forms of religion, such as the worship of the symbol of an unseen power.

It is an early product of the primitive religious instinct of humanity, developing at a low grade of culture among a people of a highly imaginative temperament.

The fundamental religious feeling which is everywhere part of the mental equipment of man has been called by Marett supernaturalism, and is perhaps best indicated in English by the term awe, in which word are implicated fear, wonder, admiration, interest, respect, even love, perhaps. The object of this religious 'sense,' or, as many would call it, 'instinct,' is the supernatural. The recognition of the supernatural, the fundamental religious feeling of awe, develops in two ways. 'There arises in the region of human thought a powerful impulse to objectify, and even personify, the mysterious or 'supernatural' something felt; and in the region of will a corresponding impulse to render it innocuous, or, better still, propitious, by force of constraint, communion, or conciliation' (50, 168).

So man personifies the power which he cannot understand, calling it by names which we translate as spirit or god, and he worships it, propitiating and conciliating it by offerings and sacrifice, and entering into communion with it by prayer. Thus are produced the two fundamental factors of religion, the belief in some mysterious power, and the desire to enter into communication with the power by means of worship. The worship of different groups of peoples expresses itself in different ways, reflecting the mental type of the worshippers, their civilisation, their culture, their character and temperament.

The cold, practical, phlegmatic Northerners worship within bare walls, while the fervour of the imaginative South demands expression in an elaborate ritual, with richness of decoration, warmth of colour, dim lights and soft music.

The extraordinarily vivid imagination and the childlike capacity for 'make-believe' of the negro, lead him further still; the lively fancy of the West African demands a visible object to which worship may be directed. He wishes really and sensibly to behold and even to possess his god, so he incorporates him in a tangible object, and satisfies his religious ardour by directing his worship to that object. Thus fetishism and the fetish are evolved.

BIBLIOGRAPHY

1. ALLEN, J. *Modern Judaism.* London : Hamilton, 1816.
2. ARMIT, W. E. ' Customs of the Australian Aborigines.' *Journ. Anth. Inst.*, ix. London, 1880.
3. ARNOT, FRED. S. *Garenganze, or Seven Years' Pioneer Mission Work in Central Africa.* London : Hawkins, 1889.
4. BATCHELOR, J. *The Ainu and their Folk-Lore.* London : Religious Tract Society, 1901.
5. BOGORAS, W. ' The Chuckchee.' *The Jessup North Pacific Expedition,* vii. (1) Leiden : Brill ; New York : Stachert, 1904.
6. BRINTON, D. G. *The Religions of Primitive Peoples* New York : Putnams, 1897.
7. —— *The Myths of the New World ; a Treatise on the Symbolism and Mythology of the Red Race of America* (3rd Ed.) Philadelphia : M'Kay, 1896.
8. BROSSES, CH. DE. *Du culte des dieux fétiches.* Paris : 1760.
9. BURTON, R. F. *Mission to Gelele, King of Dahome.* London : Tinsley Bros., 1864.
10. CASALIS, E. *The Basutos, or Twenty-three Years in South Africa.* London : Nisbet & Co., 1861.
11. CLODD, E. *Tom Tit Tot ; an Essay on Savage Philosophy in Folktale.* London : Duckworth, 1898.
12. CODRINGTON, R. H. *The Melanesians: Studies in their Anthropology and Folk-Lore.* Oxford : Clarendon Press, 1891.

95

MAGIC AND FETISHISM

13. DENNETT, R. E. 'Death and Burial of the Fiote.' *Folk-Lore*, viii. 1897.
14. DOBRIZHOFFER, M. *An Account of the Abipones, an Equestrian People of Paraguay.* London: Murray 1822.
15. ELLIS, A. B. *The Tshi-speaking Peoples of the Gold Coast of West Africa.* London: Chapman & Hall, 1887.
16. —— *The Yoruba-speaking Peoples of the Slave Coast of West Africa.* London: Chapman & Hall, 1894.
17. ELLIS, W. *Polynesian Researches.* London: Fisher, Son & Jackson (2nd Ed.), 1831.
18. ELWORTHY, F. T. *The Evil Eye.* London: Murray, 1895.
19. FLETCHER, ALICE C. 'The Import of the Totem.' *Report Am. Assoc. Advanc. Sci.* (Detroit Meeting, 1897); also 'Notes,' etc. (Buffalo Meeting, 1896).
20. FRAZER, J. G. *The Golden Bough; a Study in Magic and Religion.* (2nd Ed.) London: Macmillan & Co., 1900.
21. —— *Lectures on the Early History of the Kingship.* London: Macmillan & Co., 1905.
22. FRIEDEL, E. '*Brandenburgia*'; *Monatsblatt der Gesellschaft für Heimatkunde der Provinz Brandenburg zu Berlin,* xii. 1904.
23. GARNER, R. O. 'Superstitions of the West African Tribes.' *Austral. Ass. Rep.* 1895.
24. GASTER, M. 'Two Thousand Years of a Charm against the Child-Stealing Witch.' *Folk-Lore,* xi. 1900.
25. GREGORY, AUGUSTA, Lady. *Gods and Fighting Men.* London: Murray, 1904.
26. GUNN, JEANNIE. *The Little Black Princess; a True Tale of Life in the Never-Never Land.* London: Moring, 1905.
27. HADDON, A. C. *The Study of Man.* London: Murray, 1898.

BIBLIOGRAPHY

28. HADDON, A. C.   *Head Hunters; Black, White, and Brown.*
    London: Methuen, 1901.
29. —— *Reports of the Cambridge Anthropological Expedition to Torres Straits.*   Cambridge University Press, 1904.
30. HARTLAND, E. S.   *The Legend of Perseus; a Study of Tradition in Story, Custom, and Belief.*   London: Nutt, 1894-6.
31. HAYS, H. M.   'Hypnotism, its History, Nature, and Use.'   *Pop. Sci. Monthly,* lxvii.   New York, 1905.
32. HIRN, Y.   *The Origins of Art; a Psychological and Sociological Inquiry.*   London: Macmillan & Co., 1900.
33. HOLMES, J.   'Notes on the Religious Ideas of the Elema Tribe of the Papuan Gulf.'   *Journ. Anth. Inst.,* xxxii. 1902.
34. HOWITT, A. W.   'On Australian Medicine Men.'   *Journ. Anth. Inst.,* xvi.   London, 1886.
35. —— *The Native Tribes of South-East Australia.*   London: Macmillan, 1904.
36. JEVONS, F. B.   *An Introduction to the History of Religion.*   (2nd Ed.)   London: Methuen & Co., 1902.
37. JOYCE, P. W.   *A Social History of Ancient Ireland.*   London: Longmans, Green & Co., 1903.
38. KIDD, D.   *The Essential Kafir.*   London: Black, 1904.
39. KINGSLEY, M. H.   'The Fetish View of the Human Soul.'   *Folk-Lore,* viii.   1897.
40. —— *Travels in West Africa.*   London: Macmillan, 1898.
41. —— *West African Studies.*   London: Macmillan, 1899.
42. LANE, E. W.   *Manners and Customs of the Modern Egyptians.*   Paisley and London: A. Gardner, 1895.
43. LELAND, C. G.   *Etruscan Roman Remains in Popular Tradition.*   London: Fisher Unwin, 1892.
44. LETOURNEAU, C.   *La Sociologie.*   Paris: Reinwald, 1880.

G   97

MAGIC AND FETISHISM

45. LICHTENSTEIN, H. *Travels in Southern Africa.* London : Colburn, 1812.
46. LIPPERT, J. *Die Religionen der Europäischen Culturvölker.* Berlin, 1881.
47. *Lupton's* 1000 *Notable Things.* 1612.
48. MACDONALD, S. 'Old World Survivals in Ross-shire.' *Folk-Lore,* xiv. 1903.
49. MACLAGAN, R. C. 'Notes on Folk-lore Objects collected in Argyleshire.' *Folk-Lore,* vi. 1895.
50. MARETT, R. R. 'Pre-animistic Religion.' *Folk-Lore,* xi. 1900.
51. —— 'From Spell to Prayer.' *Folk-Lore,* xv. 1904.
52. MAX MÜLLER, F. *Natural Religion.* London : Longmans, 1892.
53. NASSAU, R. H. *Fetichism in West Africa.* London : Duckworth, 1904.
54. PINKERTON, J. *A General Collection of the Best and Most Interesting Voyages and Travels in all Parts of the World.* London : Longmans, 1814.
55. PODMORE, F. *Apparitions and Thought-Transference* London : W. Scott, 1894.
56. OWEN, MARY A. *Folk-lore of the Musquakie Indians of North America.* London : Nutt, 1904.
57. —— *Old Rabbit the Voodoo and other Sorcerers.* London : T. Fisher Unwin, 1893.
58. RHŶS, J. 'Welsh Fairies.' *Nineteenth Century,* Oct. 1891.
59. ROTH, H. LING. 'On the Significance of Couvade.' *Journ. Anth. Inst.,* xxii. 1893.
60. —— *The Natives of Sarawak and British North Borneo.* London : Truelove & Hanson, 1896.
61. SAUSSAYE, P. D. C. DE LA. *Manual of the Science of Religion.* London : Longmans, 1891.
62. SCHULTZE, F. *Psychologie der Naturvölker.* Leipzig : Veit, 1900.

BIBLIOGRAPHY

63. SKEAT, W. W. *Malay Magic.* London : Macmillan, 1900.
64. SPENCER, B., and GILLEN, F. J. *The Native Tribes of Central Australia.* London : Macmillan, 1899.
65. ST. JOHN, S. *Life in the Forests of the Far East.* London : Smith, Elder & Co., 1862.
66. STOKES, WHITLEY. 'The Destruction of Dá Derga's Hostel.' *Revue Celtique.*
67. SUPER, C. W. 'Physicians and Philosophers.' *Pop. Science Monthly,* lxvii. New York, 1905.
68. SWETTENHAM, F. A. *Malay Sketches.* London : Lane, 1895.
69. TAYLOR, R. *Te Ika a Maui.* London : Macintosh, 1870.
70. TYLOR, E. B. *Researches into the Early History of Mankind and the Development of Civilisation.* (3rd Ed.) London : Murray, 1878.
71. —— *Primitive Culture.* (2nd Ed.) London : Murray, 1873.
72. WESTERMARCK, E. 'The Magic Origin of Moorish Designs.' *Journ. Anth. Inst.,* xxxiv. 1904.

Printed by T. and A. CONSTABLE, Printers to His Majesty
at the Edinburgh University Press

For EU product safety concerns, contact us at Calle de José Abascal, 56–1°,
28003 Madrid, Spain or eugpsr@cambridge.org.

www.ingramcontent.com/pod-product-compliance
Ingram Content Group UK Ltd.
Pitfield, Milton Keynes, MK11 3LW, UK
UKHW012337130625
459647UK00009B/343